NICK PARSONS is an award-winning writer and director in film, television and theatre. He has a BA (hons) in Philosophy from Sydney University and is a graduate of both the Australian Film, Television and Radio School and the National Institute of Dramatic Art. He has directed more than a dozen stage plays, three short films, television drama, a documentary series and a feature film. He has written three produced full-length stage plays, a stage musical, several one-Acters, two feature films and numerous episodes of television series and serials. He is also the author of several radio plays.

In 1993 his play *Dead Heart* premiered at NIDA and subsequently won the AWGIE for Best Stage Play, the NSW Premier's Literary Award for best script and the Australian Human Rights Award. He wrote and directed the film adaptation of *Dead Heart* in 1996, which was nominated for the AFI for Best Adapted Screenplay and won the Film Critics Circle Award for Best Adapted Screenplay. His other screen credits include 'The Saviour', a half-hour episode of the series *two Twisted*, screened on the Nine Network in 2006, and *Tipping Point*, a 16-part mini-doc series for The Weather Channel. He also wrote three episodes of the children's TV series *My Place* Season One (2010) and one episode of season two (2012). Both series won the Logie for Best Children's TV series and Nick's episode for Season Two won the AWGIE for Best Episode of Children's Drama. He wrote five episodes of the crime drama series *The Straits* (2013), winner of the AWGIE for best TV Drama Series and the Deadly Award for Best TV Series. In 2008 Nick's play *Hollow Ground* was performed in Hobart by the Old Nick Theatre Company. The same year he directed a sold-out season of a new play by Tony Zeane, *Burnt*, for La Mama Theatre in Melbourne, and his musical *A Nasty Piece of Work* premiered at the New Theatre in Sydney.

Nick is currently developing several theatre, TV and film projects.

For
Brian Syron,
who provided the inspiration

John Clark,
who provided the means

Joanna Arrowsmith,
who showed me the way

and

my father,
who gave me many things

DEAD HEART

THE PLAY

NICK PARSONS

Currency Press, Sydney

First published in 1994 by
Currency Press Pty Ltd,
PO Box 2287, Strawberry Hills NSW 2012
in association with
Black Swan Theatre, Perth
and Belvoir Street Theatre, Sydney
Reprinted 2003, 2008
This revised edition published in 2015.

In accordance with the requirement of the Australian Media and Entertainment
Arts Alliance, Currency Press has made every effort to identify, and gain
permission of, the artists who appear in the photographs which illustrate this play.

Cataloguing-in-publication data for this title is available from the National
Library of Australia website: www.nla.gov.au

Cover image shows: Kelton Pell, Kevin Smith and Peter Francis, in the 1994
Belvoir Street production. Photo by Elise Lockwood. Cover design by Kate
Florance.

Currency Press acknowledges the Traditional Owners of the Country on which
we live and work. We pay our respects to all Aboriginal and Torres Strait
Islander Elders, past and present.

Contents

Author's note

I want to make it clear from the start that this is not an 'Aboriginal play'. It does not portray Aboriginal life and culture for its own sake. Rather, I have tried to show what happens when two cultures, with completely different values, come into conflict. I have tried to depict what I see as good and bad on both sides without prejudice or sentimentality.

In writing this play I have incurred a debt of gratitude to a great many people. These include in Sydney: Joanna Arrowsmith (my toughest critic and strongest supporter); Mal Read (who gave me the idea and a good deal of encouragement); John Clark, Elizabeth Butcher, Peter Cooke and Jenny Deves at NIDA; Christine Hartgill; Philip and Katharine Parsons and Currency Press and all who sail in her; Justine Saunders; Chris Connors; all those who participated in the first reading of the play including Richard Buckham, Ken Boucher, Harriet Parsons, Peter Hicks, Leo Taylor, Darren Gilshennan, Stewart Robinson, Craig Ilott, Berynn Schwerdt, Carlton Lamb, David James, Murree Bartlett, Deborah Galanos, Jenny Kent. In Alice Springs I am indebted to: Blair McFarland and Meg Mooney (who showed great kindness to a complete stranger), Rob Wenske, Ian McKinlay, Constable Dean Macdonald and Jenny Bartlett. I am indebted to everyone at Kintore, particularly: Peter Holt (who pushed my permit through), Pinta Pinta Tjapananka, Lyle Gamertsfelder, Kerry Arrabena and Nigel Carrick, Linda and Paul, Shane, Ronnie Tjampitjinpa, and, for their instinctive generosity, Bernard Campbell, Matthew West and Adrian Jurra. I am indebted to Paul and Jilau Parker for translating some dialogue from English to Pintupi, and for their generous advice on matters relating to the Pintupi. Thanks also to Dr Bogdan Hulewicz for his advice on forensic matters.

Nick Parsons, October 1992

A note on the revised edition

This edition of the play is slightly revised, bringing it closer to the film screenplay, which was written after the stage play.

Ray's speech in Act One that begins 'When my dad was a copper' has been moved from just after Ray's line 'we'll find 'im ... hung up like someone's overcoat' to replace a speech before the climax in Act Two after the line 'Don't give me that bullshit. That spooky Aboriginal bullshit. I don't want to hear it! I don't want to know'. Some additional dialogue from the screenplay has been included to link the speech to its new context.

The change means that, at a moment of existential crisis, Ray remains intent on his goal rather than becoming self-reflexive, which is truer to the character.

Nick Parsons, November 2015

Pintupi phrases

During the crowd scenes the actors may wish to ad-lib the following:

Kulila, kulila or *Yarkarri*	Listen, listen
Yarkarriwa or *Kanmanarrarri*	Shut up
Palanya mularrpa	That's true
Palalu tirru wankanu or *Palalu tirru watjanin*	That one said it bullshit

Dead Heart was first performed by the NIDA Company at the NIDA Theatre, Kensington on 12 May 1993 with the following cast:

Kevin Smith	POPPY
John Jarratt	RAY
Glen Shea	BILLY
Elaine Hudson	SARAH
Ross Hall	CHARLIE
Nicholas Garsden	GORDON/OAKS
Lance O'Chin	MANNGA
David Ngoombudjarra	TJULPU
Tom E. Lewis	DAVID
Alan Dargin	TONY
Terry Brady	LES
Jeanette Cronin	KATE

Other parts were played by the company.

Directed by John Clark in association with Bob Maza
Designed by Peter Cooke
Wardrobe Co-ordination by Sue Osmond
Lighting by Tony Youlden
Sound by Toni Glynnier
Production Management by David Gallen
Stage Management by Phillip Serjeant

Subsequently the play has been revised.

CHARACTERS

DAVID MULLER, Aboriginal, mid thirties
POPPY TJUNGURRAYI, Aboriginal, mid sixties
TJULPU TJANGALA, Aboriginal, early twenties
MANNGA TJAPANANGKA, Aboriginal, POPPY's brother in law,
    TJULPU's grandfather, mid sixties
SENIOR CONSTABLE RAY LORKIN, white, thirty to forty
BILLY CURLEW TJAPALTJARRI, Aboriginal, mid twenties
CHARLIE ROTH, white, thirty to forty
SARAH HAMILTON, white, mid thirties
LES MATHIESEN, white, about forty
KATE MATHIESEN, white, his wife, twenty-nine
TONY McKAY, Aboriginal, mid twenties
GORDON REYNOLDS, white, mid twenties
NIGEL FARRELLY, white, mid twenties
SENIOR SERGEANT WARREN OAKS, white, mid forties
THE FIRST MAN, Aboriginal, indeterminate age
THE SECOND MAN, Aboriginal, indeterminate age
ANDREW, Aboriginal, teenage
BENSON, Aboriginal, teenage
MAN, Aboriginal, mid thirties
WOMAN, Aboriginal, indeterminate age
GIRL, Aboriginal, indeterminate age

SETTING

A small Aboriginal community 600 km west of Alice Springs.

ACT ONE

A sandy, scrubby plain, night. Wind. A small spinifex fire. POPPY *appears: an old man dressed in jeans, shirt, jumper and coat. He wears a hat but no shoes. The* FIRST *and then the* SECOND MAN *enter from opposite directions. They are half naked, painted up for a ceremony.* POPPY *produces a pack of cards.*

POPPY: [*to the* SECOND MAN] You play card?
SECOND MAN: Yeah.
POPPY: [*to the* FIRST MAN] You play?
FIRST MAN: Yuwa. [*'Yes. '*] Good one.
  [*The three settle down to play a version of poker. There are no bets and no discards: they simply deal and then, with a dramatic gesture, throw down their cards to 'see' each other.*]
SECOND MAN: [*pointing west*] I been that way: Jiggalong.
POPPY: Mmm. Long way.
SECOND MAN: I go that one. [*Indicating flight*] Like an eagle. One man: I find 'im. Pull out his ribs, take his heart.
FIRST MAN: Ahhh. Finish?
SECOND MAN: Yuwa. That one finish, alright.
POPPY: Mmm.
SECOND MAN: [*pointing west*] That one die Jiggalong. [*Pointing east*] Then I go finish one Kiwirrkurra. Just to keep it even.
POPPY: [*to the* FIRST MAN] Where you been?
FIRST MAN: [*pointing north*] I been Balgo. One man: someone sing him, sing out his spirit. I been follow: track 'im, track 'im. When I find 'im he bleeding, he been drooling. He been dreaming red snake curling round him, round him. Little while he been finish. I sing to him. I take his arm, suck on it, suck on it. Pretty soon I suck out a blood. Pretty soon I suck out a stone.
SECOND MAN: Ahhh.
FIRST MAN: Someone sing in that stone to kill 'im.
SECOND MAN: Alright now?

FIRST MAN: He been alright. Now he's good.

[*They throw down their cards.*]

SECOND MAN: [*to* POPPY] Eh, look. You win. Big mob of money, eh?

[*They laugh. Pause.*]

FIRST MAN: Where you been?

POPPY: I been Wala Wala.

SECOND MAN: Ahhh.

[*They stop playing. Behind them, lights up on the ghostly ruins of Wala Wala: a ragged collection of Besser-brick and corrugated-iron buildings.*]

Finish, that place.

POPPY: Mmm. I finish that one.

SECOND MAN: You finish Wala Wala?

[POPPY *gathers up the cards and deals. Lights up on the lock-up. A man hanging.*]

POPPY: Yuwa. Too much drink. Too much petrol. Too much ghost.

FIRST MAN: Ghost?

[BILLY *enters the lock-up with a tray of milky tea and sandwiches. He sees the body.*]

BILLY: Eh. Eh, Danny! Danny! [*Calling*] Boss! Eh, Ray!

[*He puts the tray down hurriedly and tries vainly to get the body down.*]

Ray! He been ... Danny: he been—he been—he been hangin', boss!

[*He has nothing to stand on and the body is too heavy: he can't get the rope away from* DANNY'*s neck.*]

[*Running off*] Ray! You come! Danny been hangin' lock-up!

POPPY: [*to the* FIRST *and* SECOND MAN] Ghost.

[BILLY *and* RAY *enter, take down the body and lay it on the earth.* BILLY *exits, leaving the lone figure of* SENIOR CONSTABLE RAY LORKIN *staring down at the body.* RAY *lights a cigarette to steady his nerves.*]

That politpalla: he make everything go wrong way. Yuwa, I think politpalla do it.

[RAY *squats and gently smooths the hair of the corpse. The* FIRST MAN *shakes his hand to indicate that it's no good.*]

SECOND MAN: Mmm. Too much sorry business.

[*Lights up on* MANNGA *and* TJULPU, *who sit in the desert by a small fire. They are naked but for hair-string belts. Their spears and woomeras are nearby.*]

POPPY: This one Mannga, [*indicating the body*] father to that one lock-up. This one Tjulpu, [*indicating the body*] son to that one.

SECOND MAN: [*with recognition*] Ahhh, Tjulpu.

[*For the moment,* MANNGA *and* TJULPU *remain unaware of the others.* BILLY *enters with a folding stretcher. He and* RAY *put the body on the stretcher and exit.*]

POPPY: [*indicating* MANNGA *and* TJULPU] They been desert lo-o-ong time. [*Indicting several directions*] We looking that way, that way ... too much looking. Then we see smoke ... long, long way. We go Toyota, go driving, driving ... meet 'em up.

[*For the benefit of the* FIRST *and* SECOND MAN, POPPY *re-enacts his meeting. Weeping, he approaches* MANNGA *and* TJULPU *who see him for the first time.* POPPY *is griefstricken as he embraces* MANNGA, *and the two old men weep profoundly together until* MANNGA *breaks the hold, then lashes out and knocks* POPPY *to the ground.*]

MANNGA: Nyuntu wiyanu yantayanta palunya. Nyuntu ngayukyu marutju. [*'You didn't look after him. You're my brother in law, but you didn't look after my son.'*]

POPPY: No, I do it right way. I look after that one. Tjapanangka, ngali nganaku ngurrilku, nyakun nyuntu ngaparrtji mirripungku. [*'Eh, Tjapanangka, we'll find out who did it, then you'll pay him back.'*]

MANNGA: [*taking up his spear*] Ngayuku minali mirrirrngu. Ngayulu ngaparrjina mirripungku. [*'My boy is dead. I'll pay back someone.*]

[TJULPU *leaps in to restrain his grandfather. The two men freeze.*]

FIRST MAN: [*impressed*] He wild, eh?

SECOND MAN: Yuwa.

POPPY: That one Mannga: he come Wala Wala, plenty things finish ... plenty things come good. [*Indicating both men*] You: come: I tell you story this one Wala Wala Aboriginal Settlement.

[*Music. The* FIRST *and* SECOND MAN *dance and the ruins of Wala Wala burst into life as they conjure up an angry mob of men and women. It is night. The mob consists essentially of three groups:* TONY McKAY *and friends, including* ANDREW *and* BENSON; POPPY, MANNGA, TJULPU *and their extended family and friends; and a number of fence sitters who observe.* MANNGA *brandishes a large payback spear, and two women carry nulla nullas. The first two groups argue violently with one another. Some attempt to negotiate with those within their group. The fence sitters shout*

3

fairly indiscriminately. MANNGA *and* TJULPU *are now dressed in jeans and shirt, but look odd in them.*]

[*To* MANNGA, *indicating* TONY] That one get 'im drink. He drink, politpalla come, take 'im lock-up.

TONY: We were drinking, he sit down with us. I never got 'im drink. He got his own drink.

POPPY: [*to* MANNGA, *indicating* TONY] Palangku Tonylu ngalyakatingu tjurratja yungu nyuntupa katiaku. [*'That one brought drink to your son'*]. Palangku Tonylu ngalyakatingu tjurratja Wala Walalakutu! [*'That one brought drink to Wala Wala community!'*]

TONY: I can't bring no drink to Wala Wala. You shot up my Toyota! I got nothing to bring it in!

DAVID: [*running on*] Hey, hey, hey! What's going on?

POPPY: [*to* TONY] That one *my* Toyota! Mine! [*Indicating* DAVID] Government one! He give me that one.

DAVID: Hey! That Toyota's got nothing to do!

TONY: [*to* POPPY] After they took it off me. [*To* MANNGA] You spear me: go on. He still don't get no Toyota.

[MANNGA *brandishes the spear at* TONY. DAVID *leaps between them and puts a restraining hand on* TONY.]

DAVID: No! Wiya! [*'No!'*] Who got that payback spear? That stays at my place!

TONY: [*to* MANNGA, *indicating* POPPY] Palaru nyuntupa marutju! [*'That one's your brother in law!'*] Uncle to that one lock-up. He don't look after that one. He did it wrong way!

POPPY: No!

TONY: [*to* MANNGA, *pointing an accusing finger at* POPPY] He didn't look after him! Wrong way!

[TJULPU *runs forward and shoves* TONY. *A scuffle breaks out and they are separated by their respective allies.*]

POPPY: You drink along him!

TONY: I'm not bunji! You're bunji! You didn't look after him!

[MANNGA *looks at* POPPY *doubtfully. The spear wavers.* TJULPU *hesitates, waiting to take his cue from* MANNGA.]

POPPY: [*a little panicky*] No ... Ngayula palunya palya yantayanta. [*'I looked after him well.'*] I do it right way.

DAVID: [*to all*] No more! Finish! [*To* MANNGA] That one lock-up: ... he's gone now. Poppy and Tony, they've got nothing to do. Wantirriyala. Wiya kutjupa ngukatjaku. [*'Let it go now. No one's to blame.'*]

MANNGA: [*raising his spear, angrily*] Ngayuku minali mirrirrngu! [*'My boy is dead!'*] [*To* POPPY] Ngayuku minali mirrirrngu! [*'My boy is dead!'*]

> [*People start to shout excitedly.* DAVID *tries vainly to pacify them.* POPPY *looks about nervously.* RAY *and* BILLY *enter at a run.*]

RAY: [*to* BILLY, *indicating* MANNGA] That 'im?

BILLY: Yuwa.

RAY: [*indicating* TJULPU] And that's the young one.

BILLY: Tjulpu. Yuwa.

POPPY: [*to* MANNGA] He been die lock-up! [*Pointing to* RAY] That one take 'im, put 'im lock-up!

RAY: [*to all*] Alright, shut up! Shut up the lot of you! Shut up!

> [*No effect.* RAY *draws his pistol and fires into the air. Everyone dives for cover. Silence.*]

[*To* MANNGA, *indicating the spear*] You: Tjapanangka. What you doing with that?

MANNGA: Payback one. You watpalla go.

RAY: No chance.

MANNGA: Aboriginal law. You go.

RAY: [*indicating himself*] Watpalla law. I stay. [*To all*] What is all this? This Wala Wala way? You want to kill each other?

> [*Pause.*]

[*To* MANNGA] I been policeman, okay? Watpalla law. You: you want payback for that one lock-up, eh? Your son? You want payback?

MANNGA: Yuwa.

RAY: Okay. In Wala Wala we do proper one payback: we make a time and a place. We choose one fella, and you tell me: [*Indicating his head, his thigh, his calf*] you pay back here, or here ... or here. Then we all know. That's how we do it proper way in Wala Wala.

> [MANNGA *looks at him uneasily.*]

One fella. [*Holding up one finger*] One only. Okay? You pay him back, then finish. Okay? Fair enough?

> [MANNGA *looks at* RAY.]

Otherwise you go lock-up. Maybe go lock-up Alice Springs. You like that one? You choose one, okay?

> [MANNGA *hesitates, then grudgingly looks around for a victim. Some uneasy shuffling.*]

POPPY: [*to* MANNGA, *indicating* RAY] That one put him lock-up.

DAVID: Poppy!

[POPPY *looks at* DAVID *angrily.* RAY *holds his ground. Still clutching his spear,* MANNGA *slowly approaches* RAY *and looks him in the eyes.* RAY *doesn't move.*]

Ray ...

[RAY *silences him with a gesture. Pause. Suddenly* MANNGA *raises the spear and points it at* BILLY.]

MANNGA: That one.

RAY: No.

MANNGA: That one.

RAY: I said, 'No'. Not police.

MANNGA: [*pointing at* RAY] You give me one. [*Pointing the spear at* BILLY] I take that one.

RAY: I said, 'No', fuck you.

[MANNGA *takes a step back and raises his spear at* RAY.]

[*Reaching for his gun*] Hey!

[POPPY *grabs* MANNGA's *wrist and holds him back.* BILLY *jumps between* MANNGA *and* RAY.]

BILLY: Boss! It okay.

RAY: Get out of the way.

BILLY: You settle down.

DAVID: [*to* MANNGA] Not a white man! No watpalla; wrong way. You can't fight watpalla: too much shame in that.

BENSON: Eh, Ray: you can shoot 'im!

WOMAN: You can shoot 'im, Ray!

[*Nervous laughter from a few.* MANNGA *holds his martial pose.* POPPY *waves his hands angrily at the bystanders.*]

POPPY: [*to those who are laughing*] Eh! Shame one! No good!

RAY: [*to* BILLY] No, fuck off. Get the fuckin' cuffs out and put them on that bastard.

BILLY: It okay. I do it wrong way.

RAY: No, you didn't. The bastard hung himself! You had ... nothing to do.

BILLY: Aboriginal law, Ray. That one been lock-up, I don't look after him. Gotta make it even; do proper one payback. Like you say.

[BILLY *goes to* MANNGA. *The shouting dies down again.*]

Eh, Tjapanangka.

[MANNGA *looks at him a moment, then nods.* BILLY *takes his trousers off, folds them neatly and hands them to* RAY.]

RAY: Oh, no, Billy.

BILLY: Don't worry, Boss. I can make that pain not hurt.

6

RAY: No, fuck it, Billy. No. Don't do this.

BILLY: I think more better this one, eh?

[RAY *clutches the trousers as* BILLY *goes to* MANNGA. *The shouting starts up again. A circle forms around them, separating* BILLY *from* RAY. BILLY *presents his thigh. Between the spectators,* RAY *observes* MANNGA *drive the spear into* BILLY*'s leg, then lean on it with all his weight. The spear goes straight through.* MANNGA *withdraws it and drives the spear in once more. He grinds the shaft around once or twice, then withdraws it.* BILLY *wavers for a moment, then passes out.* MANNGA *steps back, satisfied. The two women with nulla nullas rush forward and begin to pound* BILLY *about the head.* RAY *can stand it no longer. He steps forward, waving his arms.*]

RAY: That's it! Enough! Finish! All finish! Leave him!

[*The crowd separates, the shouting dies.* BILLY *lies in the dirt, pierced and bloody.*]

Oh, fuck. Ahhh, Billy, you stupid prick.

[*The crowd begins to disperse as* RAY *kneels by him and touches his leg where the spear went through. He draws his hand away covered in blood.* RAY *looks up in fury at* MANNGA, *would like to speak, but bites his tongue. Instead, he stands and grabs* TONY *by the front of his shirt.* TONY *holds up a hand to shield himself from a blow.* RAY *glares at him.*]

You take him to the clinic.

TONY: Yeah.

RAY: Benson!

[RAY *releases* TONY. *He and* BENSON *haul* BILLY *up.*]

You fuckin' watch it! Just ... [*To* TONY] You should treat him real well.

TONY: Yeah.

RAY: Yeah.

[TONY *and* BENSON *carefully carry* BILLY *off.* RAY *turns to* MANNGA.]

I hope you're satisfied.

[MANNGA *nods: he is.* RAY *continues to stare at* MANNGA *until* DAVID *steps forward and puts a hand on* RAY*'s shoulder.*]

DAVID: [*to* MANNGA] All finish now, eh? You got payback: that's an end to it.

[*Their focus broken,* MANNGA *turns slowly and leaves with the*

others. DAVID *squeezes* RAY*'s shoulder.*]
He'll be okay.

RAY: Yeah.

[RAY *strides off after* BILLY, *still holding the trousers.* DAVID *is left alone, looking after him. Lights down on Wala Wala; lights up on the school classroom, the next day. The teacher,* LES MATHIESEN, *stands in front of his class. Behind him is a white marker board on which are two sentences in black: 'The door was broken. The axle was broke.' In both sentences* LES *has used red for 'was', and also for the 'n' in 'broken'. These are his corrections. He writes another 'n' on the end of the last sentence.*]

LES: 'The axle *was* broken.' Is *this* a sentence?

[*Haphazard assent from the class.*]

Good. [*To a child*] And your third sentence?

CHILD: 'That car been fucked.'

[LES *turns to the board and writes in black: 'That car'. He then continues in red: 'was'.*]

LES: 'That car *was* ...' [*Writing*] 'damaged ... beyond ... repair.'

[*An* ABORIGINAL MAN *enters. He is painted for a ceremony and carries a spear.*]

ABORIGINAL MAN: Eh.

[LES *turns and starts.*]

No school. Finish.

LES: What?

ABORIGINAL MAN: [*pointing at him, and then off*] You: inside house.

LES: Well ... why?

ABORIGINAL MAN: Business.

[*Lights down. The clang of a cell door, then the wailing of women. Nearer, dogs howl in answer. Lights up on the clinic, day. It's hot.* BILLY *lies on a stretcher, eyes closed, with his thigh bandaged.* SARAH *leafs through a book without much interest, occasionally swigging from a mug of coffee.* RAY *stands at the window, smoking.*]

RAY: Christ, I could do with a beer.

[SARAH *picks up her coffee mug, grimaces and puts it down again.*]

SARAH: Isn't there some at the station?

RAY: Yeah ...

SARAH: Well ... can't you sneak out?

RAY: Yeah ... No, better not. [*To* BILLY] I'm already in the shit, aren't I, mate?

[*No answer.*]

SARAH: Asleep.

RAY: Thank Christ.

SARAH: What time is it?

RAY: [*glancing at his watch*] Ten past four.

[SARAH *lets out a long breath: it's been a long shift. She joins* RAY *at the window, takes the cigarette from his fingers and draws back on it.*]

Thought you didn't smoke.

SARAH: [*handing it back*] I don't. I'm not.

[RAY *looks down at* BILLY. SARAH *touches his cheek lightly.*]

RAY: Will he be okay?

SARAH: Yes. I think so.

RAY: You think he'll walk alright?

SARAH: I don't know. It depends on what the ... what the surgeon can do.

[*He looks at her, then wanders back into the room.*]

RAY: I stopped a payback once. When I first came out here.

SARAH: What happened?

RAY: They got him the next day. When I wasn't around. [*Nodding to the window*] They like to get things squared up before the law men come through; if they don't it can blow up in the ceremony and the consequences of *that* ...

SARAH: [*looking at* BILLY] 'Squared up' ...

RAY: Yeah. Part of the programme.

[*Lights up outside as a* YOUNG MAN *with a coat over his head enters along a red dirt road. In the light of day Wala Wala proper is at last revealed: a small Aboriginal settlement on the eastern fringe of the Gibson Desert, six hundred kilometres west of Alice Springs. It looks like a rubbish dump; nevertheless, the sky and the startling landscape gives it an elemental quality which can't be disguised. In the foreground is* POPPY'*s old camp: a curve of corrugated iron against a derelict Toyota four-wheel-drive utility. The vehicle is missing its front doors and windscreen, and what remains is peppered with bullet holes. Occasionally* POPPY *chooses to survey his domain from the front seat of this old car; otherwise he sits on a blanket within the curve of corrugated iron.*]

The YOUNG MAN *walks around aimlessly, then settles down in the dirt. Inside,* SARAH *and* RAY *stare out.*]

SARAH: You think they'll go much longer?

RAY: Nah. I'm running the disco tonight.

SARAH: Oh, that's right.

[*Lights down on the clinic. Outside,* POPPY *enters and sees the* YOUNG MAN. *With a growl he pulls the coat off the* YOUNG MAN*'s head: he has the lip of a can in his mouth so that most of his face is covered.*]

POPPY: Eh: no good.

[POPPY *tries to grab the can, but the* YOUNG MAN *slaps him away. He yanks his coat away from* POPPY, *then looks at him indifferently for a few seconds.*]

You: shame one. Shame!

[*The* YOUNG MAN *weaves off.*]

[*Shouting*] Eh! Eh! You Tjungurrayi! That wrong way! Wrong way! You! Eh!

[*But the* YOUNG MAN *has gone.* POPPY *settles down at his camp. Lights up on the teacher's house, day.* LES *admires* KATE*'s small painting.*]

LES: Oh, that's coming along.

KATE: It's just the underpainting. It won't look anything like that.

LES: More red?

KATE: Ochre. I just want the green to show through underneath.

LES: I still think it's beautiful.

KATE: Oh, don't, Les. I hate showing things that aren't finished.

LES: I only said it's good!

KATE: [*covering the painting*] It's not anything. Please. It's not finished.
It's therapy for God's sake.

LES: Alright.

[*He turns away to the window. Pause.*]

KATE: I wish they'd finish their business out there.

LES: Ah, well.

KATE: I'm getting cabin fever.

LES: [*indicating the painting*] Wonderful subject. Where is it?

KATE: Oh ... not too far. In the Buck Hills.

LES: You'll have to show me some time.

KATE: If you like.

LES: Not if you don't want to.

    [*Pause.*]

    I think you're spending rather a lot of time on your own.

    [*Pause.*]

    You shouldn't be driving out there by yourself.

KATE: I'm not going very far.

LES: That's not the point. You can die in a few hours out there.

KATE: I'm very careful.

LES: Ted found two young men yesterday.

KATE: Oh, yes?

LES: On the way to Kiwirrkurra. Their car broke down, and they'd been there three days.

KATE: Oh, my ... Were they ... They weren't ... ?

LES: No, no. No, they were alive, but ... well, they didn't take any water with them, so they were both ... they were both crazy. They drank the radiator water, they drank anything they had. When he found them they'd just drunk the last bit of liquid they had, which was a bottle of shampoo.

KATE: Oooh.

LES: Well, Ted had plenty of water, but when they smelt it they fought him for it like ... like animals and because they'd just ... drunk a bottle of shampoo, well ...

    [*He makes a dismissive gesture.* KATE *snorts with laughter.*]

    Their mouths were—were—were—were *frothing up*—It's not *funny.* It took an hour before they were—were—were—were *rational.* It was a very ... very very very *serious* situation.

    [KATE *laughs harder.*]

    They could've *died,* he said.

    [LES *cracks despite himself and they laugh together.*]

    I rather wish you'd be careful, that's all.

    [KATE *embraces him.* LES *pats her on the back for a few moments, then abandons her and goes back to the window.*]

    You know, I don't know why ... You'd think the Aborigines, of all people, you'd think they'd know to take a little water at least.

    [TONY, *an Aborigine, enters from the living room.*]

TONY: Take it where?

LES: Oh ... when they're travelling. You know.

    [LES *continues to look out the window.*]

[*To* KATE, *affectionately*] Look at those kids.

[KATE *doesn't move from her spot.*]

KATE: Yes.

[TONY *glances from one to the other. Pause.*]

TONY: Well, *Ray Martin*'s over.

KATE: Is the movie on?

TONY: Yeah, piece of shit. I watched a bit of it.

LES: Shouldn't you be at the business?

TONY: Aaah ... Not my business.

LES: Ah.

[LES *stares out the window.* TONY *grins and moves to* KATE *until he is standing uncomfortably close. She backs away and* TONY *follows.*]

That orange brown ... and that blue ... and that olive green. Where could you find colours like that? It's ... what can you say? Elemental.

[TONY *breaks off his pursuit of* KATE *and joins* LES *by the window.*]

So harsh a place, but God, I love this country.

[*They look out.*]

TONY: Why?

LES: You know I've never been to Lake Macdonald? Why don't we all go tomorrow? It's only twenty miles. Less.

TONY: If you want, but ... it's a big salt pan.

LES: Kate?

KATE: No, I want to finish the painting tomorrow.

LES: Oh, well.

TONY: [*to* KATE] Mmm. Done a bit more, eh?

[TONY *lifts the oilcloth.*]

Good one. Green hills.

KATE: It's only the underpainting.

[KATE *grabs at the oilcloth but* TONY *keeps it out of her reach.*]

TONY: No, big mob of money for that one. Better ring the Artist Co-op.

KATE: Tony!

[TONY *picks up the phone.*]

TONY: Yo! Alice Springs? Yeah, we got a genius over here ... Yeah, true. No, white woman.

[TONY *looks at the receiver.*]

[*To* KATE] Hung up on me.

[*Off, an electric guitar starts up, played at fearsome volume very badly.* KATE *takes the cloth from him and hangs it over the painting.*]

KATE: Comedian.

TONY: Better than the shit they paint round here, eh?

[*The painful guitar continues.*]

LES: Business must be over.

KATE: He never seems to get any better, does he? The guitar, I mean.

TONY: Petrol sniffer: sound deadly to him.

[*Pause.*]

I go paint that school a bit more.

LES: Yes, alright. See you, Tony.

[TONY *exits back through the living room.*]

[*Looking after him*] Ah, he's working out very well.

KATE: Yes. Yes, he is.

LES: You were dubious, I remember.

KATE: Yes, I was.

LES: No cause for complaint now, though.

KATE: No. No, none.

[LES *smiles victoriously. Lights down on the teacher's house; lights up on* RAY *and* SARAH *in the clinic. The guitar continues.* CHARLIE *enters with* RAY*'s coat bundled under his arm. He unrolls it on the table and takes out four cans of VB.*]

SARAH: You're an angel.

CHARLIE: Contraband.

RAY: Thanks, mate.

CHARLIE: [*opening a can*] Pray the cops don't spring us.

BILLY: Mmm. Beer.

RAY: Oh, you're awake now?

SARAH: [*to* BILLY*, patting his hand*] No, no. Not for you, sport.

[RAY *and* SARAH *grin at each other as they crack their beers.*]

CHARLIE: Hey, palya, Billy? [*'Are you well, Billy?'*]

BILLY: Yuwa.

CHARLIE: Good on you.

SARAH: How was the ceremony?

CHARLIE: Oh ... I was face down in the dirt for most of it. With all the other women and children. [*Taking out a notebook*] Which reminds me ...

[*He scribbles a note.*]

13

Frustrating for an anthropologist.

SARAH: Ronnie says he'll teach me to be ngankarri.

CHARLIE: [*still writing*] Good ...

SARAH: I'd like to know about ... traditional medicine.

RAY: Yeah, gotta watch it when they start ... [*'teaching you things.'*]

SARAH: Start what?

RAY: Well, you don't want to get tied up to one group, you know?

SARAH: I'll be alright.

RAY: Okay; just I've seen it before. It's always the white bastard that gets pissed on. I wouldn't even take a skin name.

SARAH: Really?

RAY: No, half the blokes I collard'd be a relative. I'm not winning Best and Fairest as it is.

SARAH: Yes, I know. I'll watch my ...

> [*A light plane passes overhead.* RAY *and* SARAH *watch through the window as it lands.*]

RAY: That's it.

SARAH: I'll bring the car round. [*Handing her can to* RAY] You better take this.

CHARLIE: I'll come with you.

RAY: [*to* SARAH] Yeah, thanks. Billy: ... you ready?

> [*No answer.* RAY *taps him on the cheek.*]

Hey. Billy?

BILLY: Mmm?

RAY: You okay?

BILLY: Right as rain.

RAY: Good on you.

BILLY: You give me beer.

SARAH: [*smiling*] He's alright.

> [SARAH *and* CHARLIE *exit.* RAY *stares at* BILLY *a moment, a beer in each hand.*]

RAY: We're gunna take you to the airstrip.

BILLY: Mmm.

RAY: You'll have a holiday, you brave bastard.

BILLY: Good one.

> [*Pause.*]

RAY: You know ... Billy?

BILLY: [*groggily*] Yeah ...

RAY: In Alice ... maybe someone—some ... police fellas ... might come and ask you ... if I did everything I could to—to prevent what happened. With Danny. You know: to prevent how he ... how he hung himself.

[*Pause.*]

I mean I liked him; I thought he was a good bloke. I thought it was a shame he died.

[RAY *looks down at him, then shakes his arm gently.*]

Billy?

BILLY: Yeah.

RAY: What d'you think? You think I did everything I could?

BILLY: Yeah.

RAY: Yeah, me too.

[*He swigs his can. Pause.*]

You think I drink too much?

BILLY: No.

RAY: No, me neither. No, stone cold sober most days. Not like Danny, eh?

[*Pause.*]

I said, 'Not like Danny, eh?'

BILLY: Mmm.

RAY: No. No, his state was far from sober.

BILLY: That one been violent and abusive.

RAY: That's right.

BILLY: [*indicating his eye*] He punch you that one.

RAY: Yeah, he did.

[*Pause.*]

But I didn't crack. I was stone sober.

BILLY: Yuwa.

[RAY *puts one of the VBs in* BILLY's *hands, then pats him on the shoulder.*]

RAY: Yeah, Billy Boy. Have a go at that one.

[BILLY *raises the beer a little shakily, then lowers it again.*]

BILLY: Boss.

RAY: What?

BILLY: You been look out, okay?

RAY: Look out? Why?

[BILLY *shrugs.*]

Why? What's up?

[*Pause.*]

I'll be right.

BILLY: Yuwa. Okay.

RAY: You don't try anything with me, Billy Boy.

BILLY: Try something with you, wind up in the shit.

[*Lights down on the clinic; lights up on Wala Wala, Sunday morning.* POPPY *regards the settlement from his regal position in the front seat of his Toyota.* CHARLIE *leans on the door, next to him. Several people drift past on their way to church.*]

CHARLIE: [*as casually as possible*] That fella Mannga: he's your bunji [*'... brother in law ... '*], that one.

[*No response.*]

Strong fella. I like to meet that one.

[POPPY *looks at him.* CHARLIE *waits.*]

POPPY: You write that one.

CHARLIE: In my book. Maybe.

POPPY: Mmm.

[DAVID *enters, also going to church. He is resplendent in full vestments and waves cheerily to one or two of his flock.* POPPY *continues to* CHARLIE.]

You been here long time.

CHARLIE: One year: little bit long time.

POPPY: You know little bit law. I talk, you hear, eh?

CHARLIE: That's true.

POPPY: [*indicating two individuals*] I talk that one, that one: they been not hear me. Not sit down quiet. I don't tell that one law: [*Tapping his chest*] I keep it here. [*Pointing to* CHARLIE] You hear me right way: you sit down proper one. Now I tell you little bit secret law.

CHARLIE: [*delighted*] Okay. Okay, Poppy. Good one.

POPPY: You my friend.

DAVID: [*calling*] Eh, number-one singer, you coming?

POPPY: Yuwa. [*To* CHARLIE] You come.

CHARLIE: Eh, no. Church: that's not for me. Okay?

[POPPY *looks at him, then slaps him cheerfully on the shoulder.*]

POPPY: Okay.

[POPPY *jumps down and follows* DAVID. CHARLIE, *full of excitement, exits in the opposite direction.*]

DAVID: You talk to Charlie, eh?

POPPY: Mmm. [*Glancing after him*] Silly bugger.

> [DAVID *glances at him but says nothing.* POPPY *turns back to him.*]
> You: give me Toyota.

DAVID: Eh, no Tjungurrayi.

POPPY: You write letter. Government.

DAVID: [*indicating the derelict vehicle*] No, no. You smash up that one.

POPPY: [*outraged*] No!

DAVID: I get you one next year. Maybe next year.

POPPY: That Toyota mine. [*Waving a hand in the direction of the teacher's house*] You say: not his one: mine.

> [DAVID *stops and turns to him.*]

DAVID: That's right. Tony did that wrong way. It wasn't his.

POPPY: Government give it me.

DAVID: Yep, true.

POPPY: [*pointing at the teacher's house*] Grog runner, eh?

DAVID: Yeah, Govenment took it off him, gave it to you. But he didn't know that. He come here to be teacher's aide and he saw that Toyota: he thought it was still his.

POPPY: That one mine!

DAVID: Yeah, true. But Tjungurrayi, you got a rifle and shot that Toyota to bits.

POPPY: Yuwa.

DAVID: And you smashed all the windows.

POPPY: Yuwa. Big fight.

DAVID: That's no good. Big mob of money, that Toyota.

POPPY: That *my* Toyota! Mine!

DAVID: That's right. And you shot it to bits.

POPPY: Yuwa. You get me 'nudder one.

DAVID: I can't.

POPPY: Government.

DAVID: No. I can't. Maybe next year. You got a big fine for shooting up that Toyota. Ray sent you Alice Springs: remember? I can't get you another one yet.

POPPY: [*looking at the policeman's house*] Yuwa. Fuckin' bastard.

DAVID: [*angrily*] Eh, Tjungurrayi! Sunday.

> [POPPY *looks a little sheepish, but ploughs on.*]

POPPY: [*pointing to the policeman's house*] You: tell that one go.

DAVID: Ray?

POPPY: Yuwa. Politpalla.

DAVID: Hey, no ... Look, Poppy, I've got nothing to do.

POPPY: You: write letter. That one go.

DAVID: Nothing to do. That's between you and him, that Toyota.

POPPY: Wiya. That one finish lock-up: politpalla go.

DAVID: No, no, no. That's all finished now. Mannga got payback: finish.

POPPY: Politpalla did that wrong way. You write Land Council.

DAVID: Poppy, this one's white law. Okay? Coroner said he did it right way. I've got nothing to do.

POPPY: Someone spear him. Better that one go.

DAVID: Spear him? Who?

POPPY: Someone.

DAVID: Mannga?

POPPY: Someone. You tell him: better that one go.

[*Pause.*]

DAVID: Ray's been here long time. He's good friend to plenty people here.

POPPY: [*evenly*] Politpalla fuckin' bastard.

[LES *passes on his way to church.* DAVID *smiles and nods to him.*]

DAVID: [*to* LES] Kate not with us today?

LES: No, no. Not today.

[LES *hurries on. It's a sore point.* DAVID *turns back to* POPPY.]

DAVID: Poppy: you talk to Council. You tell Tjuppurrala. Or Wishbone. They tell me to write a letter, I write letter.

POPPY: That one go?

DAVID: I write to police in Alice Springs. They tell Ray to go.

POPPY: [*grinning*] Alright.

DAVID: You tell Wishbone.

POPPY: Yuwa. Alright. You my friend.

DAVID: Yeah.

[DAVID *goes off to church.* POPPY *is about to follow when he notices the* FIRST *and* SECOND MAN *observing. The former carries a spear. Lights down on Wala Wala, lights up on the spinifex fire.*]

FIRST MAN: Mannga spear that politpalla, eh?

SECOND MAN: He make trouble, that fella.

FIRST MAN: Yuwa.

POPPY: No ... that one make no trouble. Trouble coming this one ...

[POPPY *takes the spear and draws concentric circles in the dirt. He then draws a line out from the circles.*]

18

This one watpalla woman. Go, go, go, go ...

[KATE *enters, following the point of the spear. She wears a hat and a light dress with a low back and bare arms.* POPPY *brings the line to an end. Lights up on a waterhole by the base of a cliff, day.* KATE*'s small painting stands on its easel next to the paints. There is a blanket and a bag of odds and ends. Unlike Wala Wala, the waterhole is very beautiful.* KATE *works on the painting.* POPPY *returns to the circles.*]

[*Drawing another, parallel, line*] This one Aboriginal man. This one go, go, go, go.

[TONY *enters.* POPPY *brings this line together with the end of* KATE*'s line to indicate a meeting.* TONY *approaches the waterhole scene and sits, watching* KATE. POPPY *draws a small group of circles at the conjunction.*]

Big shame one. Big trouble coming.

[POPPY *nods gravely. The* FIRST *and* SECOND MAN *frown, take handfuls of sand and trail them as they and* POPPY *exit. Lights down on the fire.* TONY *watches silently for a few moments.*]

TONY: How old are you?

KATE: Why?

[TONY *shrugs.*]

I'm twenty-nine. How old are you?

[TONY *shrugs.* KATE *smiles.*]

TONY: You got no kids.

KATE: No.

TONY: How old is Les?

KATE: He's forty.

TONY: Uh. That's blackfella way: get 'em young. I got a girl promised me. She be fourteen soon.

KATE: Will you marry her?

TONY: Yeah, maybe. She back in Jiggalong. Still gotta have a bit of fun yet, eh?

[KATE *looks at him, smiles, keeps painting. He grins back.*]

Les, he want kids, eh?

KATE: Yes.

[*Pause.*]

Sometimes at night I can hear kids.

TONY: Yeah?

KATE: Yes. I don't know. There's a gang, or ... I hear them running around the house at night. Do you ever hear them?

TONY: Mmm. Sometimes.

KATE: They keep ... they keep breaking in while we're at school. I've talked to Ray about it, but what can you do? We can't stay home all day.

[*Pause.*]

We come home and there's ... things everywhere. Personal things. My—My—My—My underwear ... They mean no harm, but ... And they take things that ... like my grandma's wristwatch. We found it later in the dirt somewhere. I found her earring in the driveway.

[*Pause.*]

TONY: They wanna look at it.

KATE: You don't understand. That was my grandma's jewellery.

[TONY *looks at her.*]

I'm sorry.

[*She continues to paint.*]

I wish I could fit in. I ... In school I ... *make* myself wipe their noses ... Les just does it; it doesn't seem to ... to bother him, but ... the rubbish everywhere ... My mother would've *never*—My mother would've taken one look and driven straight back to Sydney.

[*Pause.*]

I'm sorry: I'm being rude.

[TONY *shrugs.*]

You can't get anything *clean* here. It really ...

[*Pause.*]

You must think I'm awful.

TONY: You getting red. You want some cream?

KATE: Oh ... Thanks.

[TONY *stands, goes to the bag and takes out a tube of block-out cream.* KATE *holds out her hand for the tube, but* TONY *squirts cream on her wrist instead. He smooths it into her arm.*]

It's beautiful here.

TONY: Yeah, pretty one.

KATE: How did you find it?

TONY: I'm looking after it. [*Pointing off, along the face of the cliff*] Round there we got business on.

KATE: Oh ...

TONY: We got big ground painting, tjuringa shield, big pearl shell.

[KATE *is suddenly uncomfortable.* TONY *grins.*]

They're at another place. They be back later.

KATE: It's alright for me to be here?

TONY: Yeah, I look after you.

[KATE *looks at him as he massages the cream into her shoulder, then at their surroundings.* TONY *starts to put cream on the other arm.*]

KATE: Les ... Les ...

TONY: Yeah?

KATE: Les had a phone call yesterday from Channel Seven.

TONY: Television?

KATE: Yes.

TONY: Mmm.

KATE: Asking about the 'lost tribe'. Isn't that funny?

TONY: What lost tribe?

KATE: The ones who just arrived. The old man and ... his grandson.

TONY: They don't look lost to me.

KATE: Do you know them?

TONY: Yeah. I ran into 'em few days ago.

KATE: Les thought you might give the boy some English lessons.

TONY: English?

KATE: Yes, he's—he's—he's very much behind.

TONY: No ...

KATE: You'd get a ... a tutor's fee.

TONY: I teach that boy English, [*Prodding his thigh*] I think that old man spear me this one.

[TONY *starts to massage cream into* KATE*'s calves.*]

KATE: Why?

[TONY *shrugs.*]

TONY: Tjapanangka don't want him to learn to be watpalla. He watch his boy Danny go out drinking, go fighting, watch 'im get sick. He watch the watpallas take Danny's little boy Tjulpu, put 'im orphanage. That old man: he don't like watpalla way. He stole that boy from orphanage years ago, [*Pointing*] took him out that way. They live in desert ever since.

KATE: That's ... awful.

TONY: Yeah. Back then Government take kids all time. I grew up orphanage.

KATE: Oh. I'm sorry.

TONY: Yeah, no good. They gave me new name, everything. Didn't know who I was. When I grew up I went looking for my mother. When I found her, I knock on the door, she open up, say, 'Tony!' Then she wallop me one good. 'Where you been? What you been doing?' I'm crying, she beating me, I don't know what's going on.

[*He laughs.*]

Wish someone come and stole me back, eh? But no one come.

[KATE *looks down at him and touches his head lightly.*]

KATE: You're ... You're very bright, Tony. You could do anything, you know.

TONY: Yeah?

KATE: I mean you're not—you're not ... so tribal. You could go anywhere. Les I know thinks ... you have so much potential ...

TONY: I could study, eh?

KATE: Yes. There's a lot you could do.

TONY: Don't have to be ignorant blackfella. I could get house. Get a big watpalla job. I be boss of Les one day, you reckon?

[KATE *doesn't know how to take this.* TONY *gives nothing away. At last he points off.*]

My country's that way, my Dreaming.

KATE: But you don't believe in that. You—You told me.

TONY: Yeah, true. But ... I get lonely for my country. You stop believing one way, you don't start believing another way.

[KATE *looks at him uncertainly. Suddenly* TONY *smiles.*]

I believe you gotta have a bit of fun, but, eh?

[*His hands slide further up* KATE*'s legs.* KATE *pulls away. Pause.*]

KATE: Tony ... we have to stop this. I'm sorry.

[TONY *touches her face, then starts to undo her dress.* KATE *tries to break away but he holds her firmly. She lets him take her dress off.*]

I don't know what I'm doing here.

[*He rubs cream over the rest of her body.*]

I burn so easily.

TONY: That's nature saying, 'Go home, white man'. [*Indicating the tube*] This watpalla way of saying nature can get stuffed.

[KATE *laughs. Pause.*]

KATE: Tony: this ... I'm—I'm not coming any more. I—I—This must be the last time.

[TONY *takes some of the fine sand and pours it over her.*]
This is not what I ... what I ... Oh.
[TONY *gradually turns her completely ochre.*]
What are you doing?
TONY: Oh ... [*Grinning*] keep you safe from pankalangu.
KATE: What's that?
TONY: Spirit. He lives round waterhole like this one. We trick 'im: he don't see you're a white woman.
KATE: No. I suppose not.
TONY: He won't touch you now; he think you belong here.
KATE: Oh, God ...
[*They look at each other.*]
You mustn't ... Don't ever tell anyone, will you?
TONY: You come.
KATE: Where?
TONY: [*heading along the cliff face*] This way.
KATE: Why?
[*He looks at her.*]
TONY: I show you where we kill boys ... and make men.
[*He moves off.*]
[*Off*] Eh. Look out for pankalangu.
KATE: Tony ... [*To herself*] 'Pankalangu' ...
[*She looks about.*]
Tony?
[*Pause.*]
Tony?
[*No answer. She peers along the cliff face. Gradually she inches her way along the base and off. Silence.*]
[*Off*] No! No!
[*Silence. Lights down on the waterhole. Lights up on the muster room of the police station, day.* RAY *leans back at his desk with a cup of coffee.* DAVID *leans on the wall. Both men regard newcomers* GORDON *and* FARRELLY, *the latter clutching a Betacam case.*]
RAY: Look: you can't take pictures of a sacred site. People really get the shits.
GORDON: We didn't.
RAY: How do you know?
GORDON: Establishing shots: how could ... ?

23

[*Pause.*]

RAY: You got a permit?

GORDON: Um ... well, no. We—We ran a bit short of time for all that. It's a bit informal, though, isn't it? We could apply for one now.

RAY: [*indicating* DAVID] You better ask him: that's his job.

GORDON: [*to* DAVID] Sorry; you work here, do you?

DAVID: Yeah.

GORDON: Great. Um ... yeah, great. So ... ?

DAVID: Well, it's pretty simple. There's a form in the office: you fill it in; a Council member has to approve it.

GORDON: Right. So how long's that take?

DAVID: Depends on when we get round to it. Two to four weeks.

GORDON: 'Two to four *weeks*?'

RAY: Probably closer to three.

DAVID: I'd go back to Alice if I were you.

GORDON: That's an eight-hour drive.

RAY: You're not meant to be here in the first place. Aboriginal land, sport. It means what it says.

GORDON: They can throw us out? Legally?

RAY: They usually get me to do it.

[*Pause.*]

GORDON: Can we negotiate about this?

RAY: [*picking up the Betacam*] In fact I'll impound this right now.

FARRELLY: [*grabbing the camera*] Hey.

RAY: You can have it back on the way out.

[FARRELLY *reluctantly lets go.* RAY *takes the Betacam into the office, off. While he's there the office phone rings and is answered.*]

DAVID: [*to* GORDON *and* FARRELLY] Don't worry. It'll be safe.

GORDON: Look: the story is, we came out to do a news item: 'The Lost Tribe'; couple of interviews, we'll be here maybe half a day.

DAVID: Well, the problem —

GORDON: [*interrupting*] We'll be here and gone. We can't hang around Alice for a month. Can't you help us out?

[LES *enters, agitated.*]

LES: David, have you — ? [*Noticing the unfamiliar faces*] I'm sorry. David, I need to see Ray: have you seen him?

DAVID: I think he's on the phone. What's the problem?

LES: I've just been chased around the school by—by—by a madman wielding a—a—a hatchet like a ...

[POPPY *charges into the station.*]

POPPY: Eh! You: no good. That one no English!

LES: Oh, I think English, yes!

POPPY: No! Tjulpu no English. That one Pintupi mularrpa. ['... *real Pintupi'.*] Tjapanangka fix you proper one!

LES: He must go to school. That's whitefella law.

POPPY: No! Whitefella law no good. We teach that one right way! Aboriginal way.

[RAY *storms out of the office.*]

RAY: [*shouting*] What the bloody hell is going on here?

[*A moment of silence.* POPPY *looks at* RAY *with open hostility.*]

DAVID: Les ... Poppy ... This is ... Gordon and ... Nigel. [*To* GORDON] They're reporters from ...

GORDON: [*to* LES, *with a smile, offering his hand*] Seven Network. Hi.

LES: [*stunned*] Hello.

FARRELLY: [*offering his hand*] Yep.

[LES *shakes hands with* FARRELLY.]

POPPY: [*indicating* GORDON *and* FARRELLY] Ahhh, television.

GORDON: Ah ... yeah. [*Offering a hand*] Nice to meet you.

POPPY: You: give me money.

[GORDON *is nonplussed.* DAVID *leaps into the breach.*]

DAVID: [*to* GORDON *and* FARRELLY] What I suggest ... right now is there's a caravan for visitors back of my place. Fifteen bucks a day. You can spend the night there and head back tomorrow.

GORDON: Um ... Ah. Right. Okay.

[GORDON *hovers as* DAVID *unclips a key from his ring.*]

FARRELLY: [*to* RAY] Can I have the camera?

RAY: No. [*To* GORDON] That your four-wheel-drive out front?

GORDON: Yeah.

RAY: Petrol or diesel?

GORDON: Petrol.

RAY: Rented I guess.

GORDON: Yeah.

[RAY *goes to a locker near his desk.*]

DAVID: This is the caravan key. If you follow the road outside it's the third house on the left.

[GORDON *accepts the key as* RAY *produces a small empty paint tin with a lid.*]

RAY: Before you go to sleep tonight, fill this with petrol and leave it on the bumper bar.

GORDON: [*taking the can*] Why?

RAY: For the sniffers. Otherwise they'll bust your petrol cap.

GORDON: Oh. Right. Thanks.

RAY: No trouble. See you.

GORDON: Right. [*To the others*] Well ... nice to meet you.

POPPY: We talk.

GORDON: Um, yeah, maybe.

POPPY: [*smiling*] Alright.

RAY: [*to* GORDON *and* FARRELLY, *indicating the door*] 'Bye.

GORDON: [*to* DAVID *and* LES] And ... so ... you'll have a talk now about this guy with the axe.

DAVID: Um ... yes.

GORDON: Right. You know, what would be great—I mean, you know, um ... no chance we could ... sit in, or — ?

RAY: [*interrupting*] No. Now get out.

GORDON: Sure. Just asking. See you round.

FARRELLY: [*raising a hand*] Yep.

[POPPY *raises a hand in farewell as* GORDON *and* FARRELLY *go out to the road and exit.*]

RAY: [*to* DAVID] Those two are a big fuckin' problem.

DAVID: Possibly.

[POPPY *puts a friendly hand on* DAVID*'s shoulder, smiles at* RAY *and settles comfortably into a chair. The sight makes* RAY *uneasy.*]
Alright. Les: you want to go over what you just said to me?

LES: Oh. Yes. I ... I don't have a lot to add. I um ... I asked one of the teaching aides to ... to give Tjulpu some basic English tuition. It seemed fine. I was in class when I heard ... um, shouting. And ... I went into the staff room and there was the old man shouting at the top of his lungs and poor Melanie in the corner. When he saw me he just said, 'No school! No English!' I said, 'Yes, English'. And that's when the hatchet came out and he chased me around the school. I'm sorry; I'm still shaking. I thought ...

DAVID: But you're okay.

LES: Yes. Yes, Poppy was there and he ... he calmed things down.

[RAY *and* DAVID *glance at one another.*]

DAVID: [*to* POPPY] This one serious business, Poppy.

POPPY: That one no English. English finish.

DAVID: Okay, but Mannga can't fight watpalla. Big shame. You know that, Poppy.

> [*Silence from* POPPY.]

Now, what do we do? We do this tribal way, or watpalla way?

> [POPPY *stares at* RAY.]

Les. Will you let this be handled tribal way?

LES: Yes. Yes, as long as it's handled.

DAVID: Ray?

RAY: Maybe.

DAVID: [*to* POPPY] Okay? You punish him tribal way. That one go. Okay, Ray?

RAY: Alright.

DAVID: [*to* POPPY] Mannga go, or Ray put him in gaol.

> [POPPY *stares at him stubornly.*]

LES: But Tjulpu has to come to school.

POPPY: No. No school. Tjulpunya Pintupi mularrpa. [*'Tjulpu is real Pintupi.'*] No watpalla school that one.

LES: He needs English lessons.

RAY: Oh, for God's sake.

LES: No, that's not negotiable. He has no English at all.

RAY: Les: you're looking for trouble.

LES: Well, Ray: in that case, what are we doing here? I mean, I can't even teach English, exactly what are we supposed to be doing out here?

RAY: Les ... [*Slapping his forehead*] are you fucking going home or what? You think that old bastard's gunna get up and leave without his grandson? He's already lost his son, for God's sake.

DAVID: Alright, that's enough. Les: I don't think we can insist Tjulpu goes to school. I think Mannga should go, and I think Tjulpu should go with him. At least for a while.

LES: Well in that case I'd rather just forget the whole thing.

RAY: Well, I'm not.

LES: Well I won't press charges.

RAY: This was assault. You don't have to.

DAVID: Ray —

RAY: [*interrupting*] No. This was an assault. [*To* POPPY] You get them both out of here before it's too late. Get me? Mannga go. Tjulpu go.

POPPY: No. That one stay.

RAY: Then I take 'im Alice Springs, I put 'im lock-up, eh? You like that one?

POPPY: No, that one stay! Tjulpu stay! You go! You go, fuckin' bastard. You go, [*To* LES] you go ...

> [POPPY *turns to include* DAVID, *then hesitates. He turns back to* RAY.]

Mannga stay.

RAY: I'll give you till Wednesday. If he's here Wednesday I take him Alice Springs.

> [POPPY *stalks out.*]

DAVID: You know where he's gone now, don't you? Talk to those reporters.

RAY: Ah ... who gives a shit?

DAVID: Ray ... you're not solving the problem. We need to negotiate some form of —

RAY: [*interrupting*] 'Negotiate'?

DAVID: Yes. Negotiate. It's either that or shoot 'em. Or lock 'em up. What do you want?

LES: I'm sorry. I don't see this has anything to do with me at all. I've said I want to drop the whole thing and I certainly don't want that young boy sent out in the desert again just because of his grandfather.

RAY: Oh, get fucked.

LES: [*to* DAVID] I think that's the end of the meeting. Perhaps we'll talk later.

> [LES *exits.*]

DAVID: Ray, what d'you think you're doing?

RAY: I dunno. Tired, I guess.

DAVID: I ... am trying ... to be black and white at the same time. I'm trying to balance all the needs in this community and it's not easy. I'm warning you Ray: you're making it impossible.

> [*Pause.*]

RAY: That was Alice on the phone; hospital.

DAVID: How—How is he?

RAY: He's gunna have a limp.

DAVID: Oh, God ...

RAY: Yeah. Still, nothing odd about that, eh? Just par for the fucking course, isn't it?

[*Pause.*]

DAVID: Ray ... go and talk to Les. See if you can —

RAY: [*interrupting*] You're such a fuckin' bureaucrat, you know that?

DAVID: Yes.

[*Pause.*]

He has a legitimate position. You and I might not —

RAY: [*interrupting*] It's obvious they have to go: just look at the fuckin' place. Paybacks going on, petrol sniffers, grog runners ... The place is a fuckin' mess. Someone like Tjulpu: he'll get on the grog, he'll start sniffing, he'll just ... lose himself. I mean, what does this place have to offer? He's just like his dad. He's a nice kid, but a few years down the track he'll spend the night in the lock-up and we'll find 'im ... hung up like someone's overcoat.

[*Pause.*]

Ah, fuck. I'm sorry, mate. I'm just ... This place is fucked. You know that, don't you? Sooner or later ... it's just gunna ...

DAVID: Ray, the Council wants me to write a letter requesting you be transferred.

RAY: Oh. Right.

[*Pause.*]

Right. Well ... I saw it coming. Those pricks. You gunna write that letter?

DAVID: Have to.

RAY: Fuck it ... Fuck. How many times have I ... ? This is over Poppy's bloody Toyota, you know.

DAVID: No, it's not.

RAY: Of course it bloody is. At bottom. He has some big argument with Tony about it, shoots the fuckin' thing to pieces, and I'm the big villain because I sent 'im down for it. It was only a fuckin' fine, you know; it's not like he spent his ... you know, his life in prison. Now he's out to get me.

DAVID: That's not the reason.

RAY: Course it fuckin' is. Sometimes I wonder if you know how this place runs at all. How you gunna word this bloody letter?

DAVID: However they want.

RAY: Oh, come on, Dave.

DAVID: I'm community advisor. I have to write the letter they ask for.

RAY: Dave, come on: I've been here seven years. Seven years. You know you can write any fuckin' letter you like. You could word it nicely.

DAVID: I have to be true to the spirit of what the Council —

RAY: [*interrupting*] What about being true to me? I'm your mate, for fuck sake. I got you this job in the first place.

DAVID: I know that, Ray.

RAY: If I hadn't stood by you, if I hadn't ... hammered the Council on your behalf you'd still be running round the country spreading God's word for the Lutheran Fuckin' Church.

DAVID: I *know*, alright?

[*Pause.*]

RAY: But you'll shaft me all the same.

DAVID: You shafted yourself. I'm telling you as a favour.

RAY: You're shafting me.

[*Pause.*]

I can't believe this. You're the only real friend I've got left in this place. I thought you were.

DAVID: Why do you think I'm warning you? Listen: it's a Council request; there's been no public meeting. Play your cards right, it'll blow over.

RAY: With no help from you.

DAVID: I've given you all the help I can. It's up to you.

[*Pause.*]

RAY: Thanks, mate.

[RAY *exits into his office.* DAVID *is left alone. He prays for a moment. Lights down on the muster room; lights up on the desert, night.* TONY *warms himself next to a spinifex fire. Behind him is a utility with tarpaulin stretched across the load in the back. He has a can of VB in his hand.* TONY *watches as a car approaches and stops.* TONY *tosses his can into the scrub. The door slams.* TONY *waves cheerily.* RAY *enters.*]

TONY: Eh, Ray.

RAY: Tony. G'day.

[RAY *warms himself by the fire.* TONY *watches him.*]

Cold night.

[*Pause.*]

Long trip?

TONY: Papunya.

RAY: Oh, yeah. Been visiting, eh?

TONY: Yeah.

RAY: On your way home.

TONY: Mmm.

RAY: You lend the truck off Matthew, eh?

TONY: Yeah.

> [*Pause.*]

Uh ... What you come out here for?

RAY: Oh ... just noticed you weren't about. Thought I'd drive out, see if I ran into you. Thought you might've been to Alice Springs.

TONY: No.

RAY: You got a bit of a load on the back.

> [TONY *shrugs.*]

Your mob from Jiggalong, eh?

TONY: Yeah.

RAY: Thought so. Mate of mine works at Newman. Tom Erhardt. Remember him?

> [TONY *shrugs.*]

He remembers you. I rang him at Easter. You're a bit of a lady killer, eh?

> [TONY *grins and shrugs.*]

You got yourself in a bit of trouble over there some time back. A girl who was wrong skin, or something? There was gunna be payback and you went to the police and my mate Tom helped you get out. Remember? I don't blame you: who wants to walk with a limp for the rest of your life? Must be hard, though. Can't ever go back, can't see your own country. Aboriginal law: pretty hard, eh? I guess the kid would be five or six by now.

> [*Pause.*]

Got your licence, by the way?

> [TONY *pulls his driver's licence from his pocket and gives it to* RAY, *who glances at it without real interest.*]

And the keys, thanks.

> [TONY *hesitates, then hands over a set of keys.*]

I don't suppose there's any beer or wine on the back of that truck. Mind if I take a look?

> [RAY *turns towards the truck.*]

TONY: Ray ...

[RAY *turns back.* TONY *grins and holds out his arms in a what-do-you-want-from-me? gesture.*]

RAY: What?

[*Pause.*]

TONY: You're my friend, eh?

RAY: I'm everybody's friend.

TONY: I'm your friend.

RAY: How d'you mean?

TONY: Maybe ... someone try'n'a make you go. Someone write letter. Maybe I talk up for you at meeting. Maybe stop that letter. Maybe tell you ... what people saying. You gotta have plenty friend, Ray. You need someone who look out for you.

[*Pause.*]

RAY: Maybe you're right.

TONY: Yeah, I'm right. You don't find nothing, okay?

[RAY *exits back towards his vehicle.* TONY *watches. A car door opens, off.* TONY *reacts with horror as* RAY *enters with his shotgun.*]

Ray?

[RAY *puts several blasts through the tarpaulin.* TONY *flinches with each one. A dark liquid pours onto the dirt.*]

RAY: Here's your licence. You're lucky I don't impound the car.

[RAY *drops the licence in the dirt.*]

TONY: Ray, you fuckin' arsehole.

RAY: Yeah?

TONY: You don't stop me before.

[RAY *points the gun at him.*]

RAY: I'm stopping you now.

[TONY *is silent.*]

You have a few drinks out bush with Andrew and Benson, that's one thing. But I didn't say you could bring it in town.

TONY: I don't bring it in town. We go out bush with that.

RAY: You wanna tell me where Danny got his last drink from? You wanna tell me that?

[TONY *shrugs.*]

TONY: You drink plenty.

RAY: [*pointing the shotgun at him*] What?

[TONY *shrugs.*]

Don't bring any more grog back here. Alright? I might ring someone in Jiggalong, let 'em know where you are.

[RAY *heads towards his vehicle.*]

TONY: Eh, gimme keys.

[RAY *takes the keys from his pocket and tosses them into the darkness.*]

Hey! I gotta drive home.

RAY: You won't drive anywhere. Your licence is out of date.

TONY: How do I get home?

RAY: If you're a real Abo you'll walk.

[RAY *exits. Off, the car starts.*]

TONY: You fuckin' arsehole! It's only bit of drink. I get my mates a drink for them, that's all. You can't tell us what to do. Eh, watpalla, you hear? You can't tell us nothing!

[*The car drives into the distance.* TONY *looks after the keys, then goes to the truck, leans in and starts the motor. It runs smoothly.*]

Real Abo don't give his car keys to no politpalla.

[*Lights down on the desert; lights up on* POPPY*'s front yard, night. Off, the petrol sniffer plays his guitar badly. A community meeting is in progress, although none of the whites are in attendance. All sit around a fire except* POPPY, *who stands in order to address the group, and* DAVID *who sits apart acting as chair. The mood is one of apathy for all except* POPPY *and, to a lesser extent,* MANNGA. *A* YOUNG MAN *hangs around the edges clutching something wrapped in a blanket.*]

POPPY: Television watpalla stay. Two week.

DAVID: Everybody think that?

[*They all raise their hands.*]

Right. Alright.

POPPY: Yuwa.

WOMAN: [*to* DAVID] You open store now, eh?

DAVID: Yeah, I think —

POPPY: [*interrupting*] You write letter?

DAVID: What letter?

[*A few begin to stand.*]

POPPY: Make constable go. We get polit aide. [*To those who are standing*] Eh! You sit down, sit down.

MAN: What polit aide?

POPPY: Someone here. You sit down.

WOMAN: [*indicating* DAVID] He open up store.

POPPY: That store closed. You sit.

> [*Everyone settles back reluctantly.* POPPY *signals* DAVID *to speak.*]

Polit aide.

DAVID: Like Billy. We choose someone, police train them up for a few months, then they come back to be police aide for us.

> [*The* MAN *shrugs.*]

POPPY: Yuwa. [*To the* MAN] Maybe you, eh?

MAN: Me? Politpalla? No!

POPPY: Maybe you. You get Toyota.

MAN: Toyota? [*Grinning*] Alright. Maybe I go politpalla school, eh?

> [*Laughter.*]

DAVID: No, we don't want police aide. Ray's been number one. He's been here a long time.

POPPY: No, he bastard, that one.

DAVID: [*pointing to someone*] He fix your motorcar, eh? [*Pointing to another*] He take your little one to the doctor Alice Springs. [*Pointing to another*] He drive you to outstation, take you hunting. [*To all*] You make him go, you do it wrong way.

POPPY: He bastard.

> [*Most bear* RAY *no real malice, but no one is prepared to speak against* POPPY.]

[*To* DAVID] Meeting say politpalla go.

DAVID: [*to all*] Is that what people want?

> [*A reluctant raising of hands.*]

MAN: You open store, okay?

DAVID: Yep. Yeah. [*To all*] Store's open now. Eh, no book down, alright? Money, money, money.

> [*There is a murmur of approval as people move off to make their purchases: this is all that has been holding them at the meeting.* POPPY *goes to* DAVID.]

POPPY: You write letter.

DAVID: I will, yes.

POPPY: [*indicating the dispersing group*] Put down all number at meeting. Meeting say politalla go. You write.

> [DAVID *looks at him.*]

DAVID: I will.

POPPY: Good one. My friend.

[DAVID exits. Only POPPY, MANNGA and the YOUNG MAN remain. MANNGA calls over the YOUNG MAN and takes the blanket from him. He dismisses the YOUNG MAN with a wave.]

MANNGA: [to POPPY] You look this one.

[MANNGA unfolds the blanket to reveal KATE's painting. Off, the guitar finally stops.]

This Kuninka one.

POPPY: Kuninka one? This one?

MANNGA: Men business.

POPPY: [staring at the painting] No ...

MANNGA: Yuwa. Sacred one. [Indicating areas of the painting] Waterhole ... Mantala tree ... That one cave. Kuninka throw rock Tingarri man.

[MANNGA mimes a great impact.]

Make that one cave. That one ground painting: men business.

[POPPY is grief stricken. He begins to rock. He wails to himself and tosses handfuls of dirt around.]

[Pointing after the YOUNG MAN] That boy steal this one schoolteacher house.

[MANNGA throws the painting on the fire. Pause.]

Tony take minyma ['... woman ... '] that place, no good. One time I camp that place along Wankatja mob. Wankatja: he strong fella. Wankatjany yanu watilpa maluku. ['Wankatja went hunting kangaroo. '] He go, go hunting. Come back, plenty kuka. ['... meat. '] We eating malu ['... kangaroo ... '], ate it all up. Wankatja camp along Tjulpu, me. His mother, wife camp little way off. We all sleeping, then something come. Tjanpa, kutjupa pitjangu. ['Kudaitcha, something came. '] [Indicating the base of his spine] Something spear Wankatja this one. Kulatakululu wakanu palunya, Wankatjanya, witapi. ['Speared Wankatja in the spine. '] Spear his mother, spear his wife. They can't walk after that. I been sleeping, something say, 'This mob hunting malu my country. Tjana wiya tjapinu, tjana katingu. ['They don't ask, they just take it. '] Ate it all: meat and blood'. Wankatja: he finish then. Knock 'im down, finish. [Indicating his shoulders] I carry his mother here. Ngayula yalipiringa. ['On my shoulders. '] Tjulpu take his wife. Nganana yanu, yankula, yankula, tiwa Kiwikurralakutu. ['We were walking, walking, walking, long way to Kiwikurra. '] Long way, to Kiwikurra, we carry 'em. They live alright but can't walk now.

[*Pause.*]
I think Kuninka do that one. More better we been punish Tony. Punkuntjaku mulamulalu. [*'Punish him properly.'*] Or something come here, come Wala Wala, [*Pointing in several directions*] spear that one, that one, that one. All finish. This place finish.

POPPY: 'Punish 'im'.

MANNGA: Punish him proper one. Ngaltuprrku wiyalu. [*'No mercy.'*] Proper one.

POPPY: Nganalu pungku palunya? [*'Who can punish him?'*] We got no strong one here. We say, 'You punish 'im', that one say, 'No, I been sick'; that one say, 'Another one do it'. That one say, 'No'. Nganalu palyaku? [*'Who can do it?'*]

MANNGA: I think one can do it. We got one can punish 'im proper one.
[*The* FIRST *and* SECOND MAN *dance on with spears. One carries white ochre and paints* MANNGA's *face.* POPPY *and* MANNGA *stand and dance with them. Lights down on* POPPY's *front yard. Lights up on the schoolteacher's living room, night.* KATE *places cutlery and place mats on the dining table.* MANNGA *breaks away from the group and approaches the living room.* KATE *sets out five mats, then glances up and sees him. She gasps. He dances closer, more menacingly. Suddenly the lights in the living room go off.* KATE *stifles a scream and turns as the door opens slowly to reveal* LES *with a birthday cake and present. Thirty candles are alight.* MANNGA *exits as* KATE *sits down.*]

LES: [*singing*]
Happy birthday to you.
Happy birthday to you.
Happy birthday, dear Ka-ate.
Happy birthday to you.
[*He places the cake on the table and softly parodies a huge crowd going 'Hooray! ... Hooray! ... Hooray!'* KATE *becomes tearful.*]

KATE: You silly man. I told you not to do anything.

LES: Well ... you're thirty. We shouldn't just let it go.

KATE: But I want to.

LES: No, you don't.

KATE: I do! Don't you understand?
[KATE *stares at the cake.*]
Promise you won't tell the others.

LES: It's not a funeral, you know. It's the best time in your life coming up. At thirty you can hear the doors shutting for the first time, but on the other hand you can see the passage you've taken. And that at least is worth a cake, I think.

[*He gives her the present. She unwraps it.*]

You should think about what's in front of you.

[*She opens the present to find a warm pair of slippers.*]

KATE: Slippers.

LES: You said your feet were cold.

[*She nods and blinks away the tears.*]

KATE: Yes. Thank you.

LES: Well ... come on. Blow the candles out; they'll be here soon. [*Glancing at the table*] I invited those reporter people; hope you don't mind. I think we've got enough.

KATE: Oh, no, um ...

LES: There's five here.

KATE: Yes, I ... Actually ... I invited Ray.

LES: What?

KATE: Yes. I just thought ... I didn't think he should be—he should feel we're all against him. That's all.

LES: You invited Ray?

KATE: I just thought ... we should. It would be ... nice.

LES: 'It ...' I ... 'It would be nice'? 'Nice'? I ... I'm afraid I feel no obligation to be nice.

KATE: No.

LES: I frankly don't feel—How could you invite him here?

KATE: Les ...

LES: If he turns up I'll tell him to leave.

KATE: Les! Not tonight, please.

LES: I suppose he thinks I've forgiven him now, does he?

[*Pause.*]

How could you do this?

KATE: Can't you be a little bit generous?

LES: 'Generous'?

KATE: To me!

[*Pause.*]

I know, yes, he was rude. He lost his temper.

LES: It's not just that. It's his attitude.

KATE: They're trying to get rid of him!
[*Pause.*]
Les ... don't ruin it for me. Please?
[*He looks at her.*]
LES: Blow out the candles.
[*Outside,* TONY *enters, laughing. He stops to look through the window as she goes to the cake. As she leans over the candles she catches sight of him and their eyes lock. Pause. She blows out the candles. On the road outside a group of men enters and* TONY *is drawn away with them. Lights down on the road and up on a sheltered area away from the community, night. It is dark. Gospel singing continues in the distance.* TONY, ANDREW *and* BENSON *settle down with a cardboard box of VBs. They're all half drunk. They don't have a fire.* TONY *mimes firing a shotgun.*]
TONY: 'Pow, pow'. [*Holding up an open hand to indicate 'five'*] I bought this one carton; [*Indicating the box*] that's all I got left. It all went in the dirt.
ANDREW: Palaru tiwupu nganampa wama. [*'He shot up our grog, eh?'*]
BENSON: He bastard, that one.
TONY: Yeah, true. I tell 'im, he don't tell us what to do.
BENSON: Yuwa. We want drink, we drink, eh?
ANDREW: Nganana mukumuku wiya ngaa tjana wangkagu. [*'We don't care what they say.'*]
BENSON: Yuwa, we growed up, eh? Ngaa nganana wangkangu palun-yayatula palyrunula. [*'We say what we'll do and we do it.'*]
[*They all swig their cans defiantly.*]
[*To* TONY, *grinning*] You got ngilpi. Tjurlkura kutju. [*'... woman. White one.'*] White one, eh?
[TONY *smiles and makes a dismissive gesture. The others all laugh.*]
You bad one. Bad boy.
[TONY *starts singing and the others join in. They start to clap.* TONY *stands and dances, then stops.*]
TONY: Can't remember.
BENSON: You dance.
TONY: No, all gone. Ngayulu puluna yangkurunu. [*'I can't remember.'*]
I go lurnti. [*'... toilet.'*]
[TONY *walks into the dark. The others continue to drink throughout*

38

the following. The Gospel singing continues. In the living room the birthday cake has been cleared away and LES, GORDON, FARRELLY, CHARLIE *and* SARAH *sit around.* KATE *stands by the kitchen with a tea towel in one hand. The table is set, ready for the meal. In place of wine is a pitcher of iced cordial.*]

LES: Would anyone like another glass of cordial?

SARAH: No, I think I've had enough.

[*The others decline with a gesture.*]

GORDON: [*indicating about forty centimetres*] We've got one bunk in the caravan that high with artefacts. And the food! I can't keep the fridge full.

SARAH: The kids.

GORDON: Like locusts.

CHARLIE: That'll get you brownie points. You feed the kids and buy the art: ... you're a useful whitefella. They don't throw away the useful stuff.

GORDON: You think?

LES: Useful to them.

[CHARLIE *laughs.*]

CHARLIE: Mmm.

[*Pause.*]

GORDON: [*to* SARAH] You like it here?

SARAH: Yeah. By and large. Money's good.

GORDON: You see much violence?

SARAH: Not ... really. Comes and goes.

GORDON: Someone died a while back, didn't they? In the lock-up?

[SARAH, CHARLIE, KATE *and* LES *exchange glances.*]

SARAH: That's right.

KATE: I think we've waited long enough. I'll put dinner on the table.

LES: [*rising*] Yes.

CHARLIE: I'll give you a hand.

KATE: No, no. Well, if you like.

[KATE, LES *and* CHARLIE *head for the kitchen.* GORDON *looks at* SARAH *for a moment.*]

GORDON: Did I fart?

FARRELLY: Nup.

SARAH: [*smiling*] No ...

GORDON: I didn't mean anything. I used to cover the Coroner's Court, so ...

SARAH: They don't want to dig it up again, that's all.

GORDON: Dig what up?

[*Pause.*]

SARAH: Danny's death. What've you heard?

GORDON: Different stories.

SARAH: I wouldn't ask about him outside. Dead people are taboo here. They're 'kumunjayi': 'no-name'.

[*Pause.*]

GORDON: You see the body?

SARAH: Yes. I knew him quite well.

GORDON: Oh. Sorry to hear that.

[LES *enters with a gravy boat and condiments, sets them on the table, glances at* GORDON *and goes back to the kitchen.*]

SARAH: He hung himself.

GORDON: You sure?

[CHARLIE *enters with a jug of mint sauce.*]

CHARLIE: Someone tell you Ray did him in?

GORDON: Ahhh ... someone ... I mean, people have opinions. I don't ...

[KATE *and* LES *enter with a roast and vegetables.* CHARLIE *stands and goes to the verandah.* GORDON *and* SARAH *take the hint and follow.* FARRELLY *remains at the table. After a moment he goes to the kitchen and helps with the serving.* CHARLIE, SARAH *and* GORDON *look out into the night.*]

CHARLIE: Ray had nothing to do with it. Some Pintupi people will tell you that he did because ... they don't accept suicide or ... random acts of fate. It's not part of their cosmology; if someone dies they—they—they ... they always they find a culprit. There was a ... a boy in Kintore was blamed for his uncle's death in a car crash just because he was given a ... a lift with him.

GORDON: Uh huh.

CHARLIE: Ray's a good bloke. But he's got a job that ... that periodically makes people hate him. And when someone dies ... popularity has a lot to do with who cops the blame.

GORDON: Not exactly fair, is it?

CHARLIE: No. I don't know. I've seen a lot of different ... practices, different customs. People say, 'This is right', or 'wrong' ... well, to me it's just a habit they have. I don't make moral judgements any more. I just observe them.

RAY: Gotta make moral judgements, mate.

[RAY *emerges from the darkness.*]

SARAH: Hi, Ray.

RAY: They make moral judgements about you all the time.

[SARAH, GORDON *and* RAY *enter the living room.* KATE, LES *and* FARRELLY *enter from the kitchen with elements of the meal.*]

KATE: Ray. We're just serving up.

RAY: Kate. [*Nodding*] Les.

[LES *looks at him and nods.*]

[*To* KATE] Not late am I?

KATE: No, no.

[KATE *exits to the kitchen, followed by* LES, CHARLIE *and* SARAH. RAY *turns to* GORDON *and* FARRELLY.]

RAY: Got a message for you two: you can stay.

GORDON: Fantastic.

FARRELLY: Can I have my camera?

RAY: Yeah, hold your horses; there's a few conditions. First one is, Council has a look at every story you do here. Approve it, type of thing.

[GORDON *and* FARRELLY *look at one another.*]

FARRELLY: [*to* GORDON] Censorship.

GORDON: [*to* RAY] We accept.

RAY: And you know you don't point cameras at that hill out there.

GORDON: Yeah, we found that out.

RAY: And just be sure you get permission before you take a picture of anyone. Sometimes they get annoyed.

GORDON: And that's it?

RAY: Location fee.

GORDON: Ah.

RAY: Thousand dollars.

GORDON: Erm.

[RAY *shrugs.*]

Oh, come on, Ray: a thousand dollars ...

RAY: Don't argue with me: it's not my ... you know.

[SARAH *enters from the kitchen with a dish.*]

SARAH: Make an offer.

GORDON: To the Council?

[SARAH *smiles.* GORDON *looks at* RAY. RAY *smiles.*]

RAY: [*to* FARRELLY] Found your binoculars, by the way.

[RAY *takes out a leather strap to which one eyepiece is attached.*
FARRELLY *stares at the dangling remains.*]

FARRELLY: Thanks.

RAY: No trouble.

[LES *enters, followed by* KATE *and* CHARLIE.]

LES: Shall we be seated?

FARRELLY: Yep.

SARAH: Mmm.

[RAY *takes* LES *aside.*]

RAY: Les ... I'm sorry about the other day. We've all got our jobs and ...
I forget sometimes that, you know, other people've got theirs. Dave
thinks I was a bit out of line. So ...

[LES *stares at him.*]

LES: We'll say no more about it.

RAY: Suits me.

LES: I haven't forgotten. But I accept your apology.

[LES *turns abruptly and joins the others.* RAY *hesitates a moment,
then takes a seat.* SARAH *puts a hand on his shoulder.* KATE *smiles
at him and he grins back briefly.*]

GORDON: [*to* RAY] Must be ... tricky being white law out here.

[RAY *shrugs.*]

RAY: Yeah. Depends. You can't be too ...

CHARLIE: 'Dogmatic'.

RAY: 'Officious'. Doesn't take much to make an enemy.

GORDON: No.

RAY: I could get thrown off here tomorrow if I'm not careful.

GORDON: You worried about that?

RAY: Yeah. Every white person looks over their shoulder. We're only
here because the Council wants us here. That's why everybody works
so hard to keep 'em happy.

LES: I wouldn't say that.

RAY: Oh, it's bloody right. We're all treading on eggshells. [*To* GORDON]
They're very smart, y'see. They're hunter-gatherers, you know? And
what they've done: they've gathered a few white people; a little handful in the middle of the desert. And the thing about white people is:
you only need a few ... and they can last your whole life.

[*Pause.*]

We are—We are ... Everything we've done out here is—is—is like a coat of wet paint: if it rains tomorrow, it'll wash off. I mean, there are some real changes; the young ones have changed. Someone like Tony: you know, no one's gunna sing him to death. But if they wanted to, the tjilpi ['... *elders* ... '] could pull this whole place back to what it was. [*Snapping his fingers*] Like that. God, in the old days: ... those old men were scary. Singing all night. Magic was everywhere. They killed people. That's the thing: you might see an old bloke, see him make a painting, you know. Nice old bloke. But you gotta remember first contact with the Pintupi was nineteen ... thirty ... ?

CHARLIE: Thirty-two.

RAY: Sixty years ago. Someone like Poppy never saw a whitefella till he was seventeen. When he was in his twenties he went out on raiding parties like anyone else. If he hadn't he wouldn't still be around. He's killed people. You look at him, but you don't think of that. You don't think of him as a killer.

[*Pause. The Gospel singing continues. The* FIRST *and* SECOND MAN *dance on with fighting spears. Over the following,* ANDREW *and* BENSON, *who have been drinking throughout the previous scene, gradually pass out. In the living room everyone is still except for* FARRELLY, *who eats with single-minded intensity. Over the following even he stops and listens.*]

KATE: At Haast's Bluff one Christmas ... when we were there ... we—we were almost killed.

LES: Well, not ... That's a bit of a ...

KATE: No, we were. There were hundreds of people. Hundreds of them. The women: you could hear them in the mornings, shouting, really screaming. And the drinking started and by afternoon it was ... We didn't go outside for days. But people kept coming to the door with blood pouring down. We bandaged them up. Then the man who ran the store—Frank—he came and he was bleeding. And a crowd gathered and they wanted him; to kill him. My mum and dad were staying: they didn't know what to think. We just sat there with the crowd outside; black faces everywhere, every window. In the end they went away.

LES: But you know ... we are really doing something out here.

[*The others look at him.*]

I mean ... making a difference. Just listen.

[*They listen to the singing.*]
The next generation: they'll be ...
GORDON: What?
LES: They'll be ... something else again.
[*Pause.*]
A toast. To the cook.
KATE: Oh ...
FARRELLY: Yep.
SARAH: Yes.
CHARLIE: Absolutely.
[*They all raise their glasses. Lights down on the schoolteacher's living room. The Gospel singing continues, off, as* TONY *re-enters from the dark and sees his companions.*]
TONY: Eh. You sleeping?
[*He prods them.*]
Wake up. Eh.
[*No result.*]
You leave me alone. I can drink alone. Don't need you bastards.
[TONY *gets himself another can.*]
Don't need no one for drinking.
[TONY *sees the* FIRST MAN.]
Oh, shit.
[*The* FIRST MAN *approaches him.*]
Hey ... [*Shaking* BENSON] Benson ... Benson!
[BENSON *refuses to wake. The* FIRST MAN *comes closer and* TONY *takes off into the bush, only to run straight into the* SEC-OND MAN.]
Andrew! Benson! Benson!
[TONY *is pursued by the* FIRST *and* SECOND MAN *through weird scrubby bushland. At last he runs off. Lights up on the school-teacher's living room, night.* KATE, *alone, pops a peanut into her mouth as she clears the coffee table. She coughs, then begins to choke. After a few moments* LES *enters from the kitchen with a tea towel in his hands, concerned. She looks at him, clutching her throat. Lights fade on the living room and bushland. Lights up on the schoolteacher's backyard, morning.* TONY *lies fully dressed on his bedroll. The sound of blowies.* KATE *enters from the house.*]

KATE: Tony! Want some breakfast?

[*No response. She goes inside. A couple of people approach* TONY *and prod him.* DAVID *enters at a distance and observes. The pair is joined by two others. They stand back and whisper, then run off.* KATE *re-enters and watches the departing foursome.*]

Hey! What's happening?

[*She approaches* TONY.]

Tony?

[*She shakes him. He is limp. She rolls him over.*]

Oh. Oh. [*Calling*] Les! Les?

[*She slaps* TONY*'s face lightly, then reacts to the touch.*]

Oh.

[LES *enters.*]

LES: What?

KATE: Les, can you call Sarah? Tony's not ... There's something wrong.

LES: [*coming forward*] With Tony? What's wrong?

KATE: Just call her! Call her, please!

LES: [*retreating*] Alright, alright.

[*He exits into the house. A few people gather near the gate.*]

KATE: Tony? Tony? [*To the others*] He's cold. Tony? [*To the others*] Have you seen Dr Hamilton? Have you seen the doctor? Someone get her.

[*The others start to move hesitantly into the yard.*]

No! Get away! Get away from us! Sarah! Get away! Sarah! Where are you? No, no, no!

[*She begins to shake* TONY *violently.* DAVID *flinches at her cries.* LES *enters from the house, but keeps his distance.*]

Tony! Tony, get up! Get up! Tony, please, no ... Tony, no ... Please ... Please, Tony ... Please ... [*To the others*] Get away ... Get away from us ... Tony ...

[*The others approach closer as* SARAH *pushes through, followed by* RAY.]

SARAH: Kate?

KATE: Sarah! It's Tony; he's not ... he's not ...

[SARAH *examines* TONY *quickly.* RAY *stands behind her.*]

RAY: [*to* SARAH] What's happened?

SARAH: I don't know. No pulse.

RAY: Jesus. Kate? What's going on?

[KATE *stares at him.*]

KATE: He's not ...

RAY: Kate?

KATE: He's not ...

[RAY *looks at her.*]

RAY: Kate, go inside.

KATE: No. No, he's ...

RAY: Les! Les, get over here!

[KATE *stands dumbly.*]

[*To the crowd*] Alright, you lot. Break it up! Come on: out.

[*The crowd moves only marginally.*]

Get moving! Hop it!

KATE: Sarah?

SARAH: He's dead, Kate.

[*The crowd starts to move.* LES *approaches.*]

RAY: [*to* LES, *indicating* KATE] Get her out of here.

LES: [*gently*] Kate?

[RAY *grabs* KATE *and pushes her into* LES*'s arms.*]

RAY: Just get her into the house, Les!

[LES *grabs* KATE *firmly and drags her away.*]

KATE: No! No! No, get away! [*Indicating the Aborigines*] Don't let
them get him! [*To the Aborigines*] Get away! Les, please ... Please ...

[LES *drags her inside.*]

RAY: [*to the remnants of the crowd*] Come on, clear off. Outside. Come
on, outside.

[SARAH *is left with the body. For a moment she doesn't know what
to do. She puts her hand to her face. As the Aborigines gradually
retreat, they reveal* FARRELLY, *dressed only in underpants, with
the Betacam on his shoulder.* GORDON *stands beside him in a pair
of jeans.*]

[*To* GORDON *and* FARRELLY] You too. Get lost.

[GORDON *nods and holds up a hand to* RAY. SARAH *shakes off
her emotion, lowers her hand and looks at the camera.* GORDON
waits a moment, then pats FARRELLY *on the shoulder.*]

GORDON: [*to* FARRELLY] That'll do. We've got it. [*Indicating someone
off*] Get this bloke.

[FARRELLY *lowers the camera and follows* GORDON *off. The
Aborigines disappear.*]

RAY: Fuck!

[*Silence.* RAY *approaches* SARAH.]

He's dead?

SARAH: Yes. He is.

RAY: Ah, fuck. Ah, Tony.

[*He kneels next to the body and looks it over.*]

He never asked for this. He never asked for it, did he? Ah, Christ, this place! Well ...

[*He looks at* DAVID.]

I'm gunna make a few changes round here. If someone did this ... I won't be doing it tribal way. Not at all.

SARAH: Ray ... we should get him to the clinic.

DAVID: [*to* RAY] Don't you think it was ... an accident?

[RAY *stares at* DAVID.]

RAY: Not sure I believe in accidents, Dave. Do you?

DAVID: [*angrily*] For God sake! There's not a ... a mark on him! What can you possibly know about it? He's just ... He's just ... He's dead. Can't ... this wait? Can't you just *wait* a little bit?

SARAH: Ray ... we do need to get him inside.

[RAY *stares at* DAVID.]

RAY: Well, well.

[SARAH *stands and moves off.*]

SARAH: There's a stretcher at the clinic.

RAY: I'll give you a hand. [*To* DAVID] Make sure no one touches him, will you? Can you do that? [*Looking at the tracks around the body*] Fuck, I wish Billy was here.

[RAY *and* SARAH *exit towards the clinic.* DAVID *looks up. Lights down on the schoolteacher's backyard.* DAVID *remains, looking to heaven. Lights up on the desert, night. The spinifex fire.* POPPY, *the* FIRST MAN *and* SECOND MAN *are seated as at the beginning of the play.* POPPY *deals out the cards once again. The two men are rapt in his story.*]

FIRST MAN: That one finish, eh?

POPPY: Mmm, finish.

FIRST MAN: [*crossing his wrists to indicate 'gaol'*] That politpalla, he put you this one?

SECOND MAN: [*crossing his wrists*] Eh, you, Mannga: like this, eh?

POPPY: No! I sing that one. I sing spirit in him.

SECOND MAN: [*astounded*] You sing that one! Politpalla?

POPPY: Yuwa. [*Indicating his head*] I sing that spirit in here.

FIRST MAN: Make him silly fella.

POPPY: Crazy mad one.

> [*They continue their card game. Lights fade.*]

END OF ACT ONE

ACT TWO

DAVID *stands alone, but now holds the dead man's shoes.* POPPY, *the* FIRST *and* SECOND MAN *play cards.* TONY*'s body has been removed.*

POPPY: [*pointing off*] Doctor woman look at 'im, look at 'im, look at 'im. Ray been look at 'im. Plenty watpalla look at 'im.
FIRST MAN: They get Tjulpu; say 'Tjulpu finish 'im'.
POPPY: [*throwing down his cards*] I look after that one.
   [*The* SECOND MAN *throws down his cards victoriously.*]
SECOND MAN: Ah! Big money!
   [*The* FIRST *and* SECOND MAN *laugh to each other.*]
FIRST MAN: [*gathering the cards*] You been too clever, eh?
POPPY: Yuwa. I been tracking for 'im. [*Indicating the ground*] I been go: 'That one heel. That him.'
   [*He laughs. The* FIRST *and* SECOND MAN *back off and observe as* POPPY *takes up a tracking stance.* RAY *enters to look over* POPPY*'s shoulder.* DAVID *moves at last and goes to them, but hangs back somewhat. Lighting change to the schoolteacher's backyard, day.*]
   [*To* DAVID, *indicating the area near the gate where the crowd gathered*] No track: all big mess. But here: good one. [*Taking a shoe from* DAVID] This one heel: broken. [*Indicating a footprint*] Broken. Yuwa. He been this one. [*Lurching around*] He been all drunk.
RAY: [*to* DAVID] That seem right to you?
   [DAVID *shrugs and nods.*]
   [*To* POPPY] Thanks.
   [POPPY *looks at him with distaste, hands the shoe to* DAVID *and leaves.* RAY *takes the shoes.*]
   I'll be glad when Billy gets back.
DAVID: What're you thinking?
RAY: I think it's all bullshit.
DAVID: Ray ...
RAY: What?

DAVID: You've got statements to say he went out drinking and walked home. You stopped him yourself with grog a few nights ago.

[RAY *brushes a fly away from his face. An eerie silence.*]

It was a heart attack, Ray. That's all it was. Sarah said it happens to young men ... more than people think. It's not unusual.

[RAY *shakes his head to himself.*]

Can you figure out a way of killing someone without ... even—without even touching him?

RAY: It's bullshit.

DAVID: What is there that tells you he was killed?

[RAY *looks at him.*]

RAY: Instinct.

[RAY *brushes past him and exits. Lights up on the doctor's living room and kitchen, early evening. On the wall is* CHARLIE*'s colourful Dreaming map of all the stories in the region. The dining table is covered by a sheet of plastic.* CHARLIE *is at work in the kitchen carving up huge chunks of meat. He drops the slices into three eskies.* SARAH *sits outside the front door with* KATE. DAVID *starts to leave and encounters the* FIRST *and* SECOND MAN. *He glances at them warily, then exits. The two men look at each other, and follow him. Lights down on the school teacher's backyard.* SARAH *puts a hand on* KATE*'s arm, then leaves her and enters the house.* KATE *stares out into the shadows.*]

SARAH: Hi.

CHARLIE: Hi. How's it going?

SARAH: Oh ... okay.

[*She takes out a packet of cigarettes.*]

I started smoking again.

CHARLIE: You'll give up. Soon as things settle down.

SARAH: God you're good.

[*She eases herself into a chair and lights up.*]

CHARLIE: Cup of tea?

SARAH: Oh, please.

[CHARLIE *drops his knife and puts on the kettle.*]

This place smells like an abbatoir.

CHARLIE: Yeah. How's Kate?

SARAH: Not great. I gave her a few Mogadon. Just needs company, I think.

CHARLIE: God, she's taken it badly.

SARAH: Well ... I wouldn't like to find you dead one morning.

CHARLIE: Oh, sure, but that's not quite ...

[*The penny drops.*]

SARAH: My God. Some anthropologist.

CHARLIE: What d'you mean?

SARAH: You're not much good at observation.

CHARLIE: She was having an affair?

SARAH: Of course she was having an affair.

[*Pause.*]

CHARLIE: Kate?

SARAH: Yes.

CHARLIE: With Tony?

SARAH: Yes.

[*Pause.*]

CHARLIE: Just ... surprising.

SARAH: Not when you think about it.

CHARLIE: But she doesn't look ... like ...

SARAH: She looks *exactly* like.

CHARLIE: Like what?

SARAH: Like ...

[SARAH *smiles and gestures expansively.*]

You know. All that eye contact.

[CHARLIE *is stumped.*]

CHARLIE: I must be the last to know.

SARAH: Not quite the last.

CHARLIE: Oh yeah.

SARAH: And don't you tell him.

CHARLIE: Me? Why would I do that?

SARAH: I know men.

CHARLIE: Do you?

SARAH: Yes. Where's my tea?

CHARLIE: Coming, dear. [*To the tune of 'Louis the Fly'*] Straight from abat-toir to you.

[CHARLIE *brings the tea to her.*]

SARAH: [*taking the tea*] Ohhh, thanks. God, your hands pong.

CHARLIE: Sorry.

[*She sips as* CHARLIE *wanders over to the Dreaming map. Outside,* RAY *enters and sees* KATE.]

51

SARAH: Ray has to drive the body in tomorrow. It's in the bulk freezer at the store.

CHARLIE: What?

SARAH: Between the kangaroo tails and the Paddle Pops.

CHARLIE: You're kidding.

SARAH: No, I'm not. There's nowhere else for it.

CHARLIE: Eeeah. Don't feel quite the same about frozen meat, now.

SARAH: That's a shame.

CHARLIE: [*looking at the eskies*] Mmm.

SARAH: I said the most likely cause was coronary occlusion.

CHARLIE: Tony?

SARAH: Yeah.

CHARLIE: Was it?

SARAH: Well, I'm sure. Probably. It's just ...

CHARLIE: What?

SARAH: Something Kate said. I shouldn't tell you.

[*Pause.*]

CHARLIE: It's up to you.

SARAH: It's in confidence, but ... it worries me.

[*Lights down on the living room and kitchen; lights up on* KATE, *sitting just ouside.* RAY *enters and approaches her.*]

RAY: Hi. Went looking for you round your place.

[KATE *looks at him.*]

Truth is I want to ... I need to ask a few more questions.

[*She stares at him.*]

I don't think ... he died of a heart attack. Did he?

[*She continues to stare.* RAY *controls his frustration.*]

Kate ... are you frightened about something? Is that it? If you are you have to tell me. Otherwise I can't help. Alright? Now ... I—I—I saw ... how you felt about him. I know ... he was more than a friend. Wasn't he?

[KATE *looks at him, hesitates, leans forward about to speak, then sees* LES *enter and approach. She looks at* RAY, *turns and escapes into the house.* RAY *looks around, sees* LES *and swears under his breath.*]

Hi, Les.

LES: Hello.

[*Together they enter the living room. Lights up on the doctor's living room and kitchen as* SARAH *opens a window.* CHARLIE *is back at his butchering.* KATE *sits quietly by herself.*]

SARAH: [*to both*] Hi. I'll try and get this smell out.

CHARLIE: Some of the boys went shooting yesterday.

LES: Ah.

CHARLIE: They gave us a coupl'a legs. I've been butchering all afternoon. [*Holding up two camel fetlocks, with platter feet attached*] I'm sure there's something exotic I can do with these.

SARAH: Charlie ...

CHARLIE: I thought that would appeal to your gourmand's palate.

SARAH: God help me. [*To* LES *and* RAY] There's more than we can handle if you'd like some.

LES: Oh, I think we're alright.

RAY: Thanks anyway.

CHARLIE: I've made some tea.

LES: That'd be very nice, thank you.

SARAH: [*to* CHARLIE] I'll get it. You wash up.

[CHARLIE *goes back to the kitchen and washes his hands.* SARAH *folds up the blood-stained plastic and follows him. Outside,* BILLY *enters with a slight hobble and approaches the house.*]

[*To* LES] Is everything sorted out at school?

LES: Oh, yes. I've taken Tony's name off all his books and his photo off the board. He's just ... vanishing from everything.

[*There is a knock and* BILLY *enters.*]

BILLY: [*cheerily*] Eh! I been *here*!

RAY: Well ... what about this bloke, eh?

SARAH: Hey ...

[SARAH *rushes out of the kitchen and takes his hand.* LES *smiles briefly, then turns to* CHARLIE*'s Dreaming map.*]

RAY: When you get back?

BILLY: Right now.

SARAH: How're your legs?

BILLY: [*slapping them*] Oh, good one. Right as rain. I play football soon.

CHARLIE: You running fast by then, eh?

BILLY: No, I been walking. They slow down for me.

RAY: They treat you right in hospital?

BILLY: Yuwa, number one. My cousin come over: we play card. Watch TV. I been have holiday.

RAY: Yeah, you lazy bastard. Plenty work around here.

[CHARLIE *brings out two cups of tea and gives one to* LES.]

BILLY: Yuwa. Too much. [*Pointing at* LES*'s cup*] Eh. You got tjampita yantjangka. [*'... cup of tea.'*]

SARAH: Oh. Yes. Would you like one?

BILLY: Yuwa, good one.

CHARLIE: Ray? Coffee?

RAY: Yeah.

SARAH: I'll get it.

CHARLIE: Ha. Promises.

[SARAH *goes to the kitchen.* CHARLIE *gives* KATE *her tea.*]

[*To* KATE] Here you go.

KATE: Thank you.

[*He puts a hand briefly on her shoulder. She reacts to the smell.* CHARLIE *doesn't notice.*]

LES: [*indicating the Dreaming map*] This is coming along.

CHARLIE: Oh, yeah. I haven't got a quarter of it.

RAY: On the inner now, are you?

CHARLIE: Well ... it seems that way. When Mannga got here, it ... Poppy seemed to change his attitude.

RAY: Oh, yeah.

CHARLIE: It's like this ... he's opened up this *world*.

RAY: Well, he's not the most riveting blackfella in town, now, is he? Gotta lift his game.

LES: [*to* CHARLIE*, pointing*] So where are we? That's Wala Wala there, is it?

CHARLIE: Yeah. [*Pointing*] Kintore's here and that's Kiwirrkurra. Most of it I can't tell you about. That purple line: that's Tingarri Dreaming.

RAY: [*pointing to an intersecting line*] So, that's ... what? That's Kuninka there.

CHARLIE: That's right ...

RAY: [*indicating the intersection of the stories*] That's where they fight, eh, Billy?

BILLY: They finish his little fella.

CHARLIE: Yep. And that's where Kuninka kills himself. Out of grief. I've got notebooks full of ... the most fantastic stuff.

SARAH: Which I'm not allowed to read.

CHARLIE: No, that's right.

RAY: Is it all going in the book?

CHARLIE: Well ... no. Not that part. It can't. Of course.

[*A slight, awkward pause.* CHARLIE *steals a glance at* KATE.]

BILLY: [*running his finger along the map*] Oooh. Waterhole. Mmm. No dot.

CHARLIE: No. No dots. Lines.

BILLY: Dot painting more better.

CHARLIE: Yeah, maybe.

KATE: [*putting down her tea*] Excuse me. I must ...

[*She exits through the kitchen into the house.* RAY *looks after her. Pause.*]

LES: You were saying?

CHARLIE: Oh. Nothing really.

[SARAH *stands and follows* KATE *off. The three men look after her. The faint murmer of conversation.* CHARLIE *and* LES *turn to contemplate the map.*]

Where's your Dreaming, Billy?

BILLY: Not here. I got Tiger Dreaming.

CHARLIE: Tiger?

BILLY: Yeah. You know: Richmond.

[CHARLIE *and* LES *laugh.* RAY *smiles: he's heard this before.* BILLY *is surprised, then annoyed.*]

What you laughing?

CHARLIE: I'm sorry. I'm sorry.

BILLY: You watpalla funny bugger.

CHARLIE: I know. I know, I'm sorry.

[CHARLIE *controls his laughter. Suddenly they are aware that* LES *is sobbing into his hands. He controls himself, then looks around at the others.*]

LES: [*to* CHARLIE] I think we'll be getting along, if you don't mind.

CHARLIE: Stay if you want, Les.

LES: No, no. I think I'd rather just pop off home.

[*He drains his tea.* KATE *appears in the kitchen and looks at him.* SARAH *enters behind her and moves into the living room.*]

Oh. Sweetheart, I was just saying we might pop off home.

KATE: Were you, darling?

[KATE *goes to* LES, *looks into his eyes, and brushes a hand across his cheek. Her hand leaves an imprint of camel blood. She turns and walks out.* LES *wipes his face with a handkerchief.*]

LES: You spend your whole life ...

[*He looks around at the others, then follows* KATE. *Pause.*]

RAY: What set that off?

[SARAH *glances at* CHARLIE.]

SARAH: I'm ... not sure.

RAY: Why? What she say to you?

SARAH: Nothing.

RAY: She said something: I could hear her.

SARAH: It wasn't important. It was just personal stuff.

RAY: Come on, Sarah: what'd she say?

CHARLIE: Ray ...

RAY: What?

CHARLIE: You're acting like a policeman.

RAY: I am a policeman.

CHARLIE: She doesn't know anything.

[RAY *stares at him.*]

RAY: Doesn't she? What about you?

[CHARLIE *hesitates.*]

Come on. Come outside.

CHARLIE: What?

RAY: Come and have a chat. Come on. Billy, stay with Sarah.

[RAY *goes outside and waits.* CHARLIE *shakes his head and follows.* SARAH *remains with* BILLY.]

CHARLIE: Ray ... there's nothing to discuss.

RAY: What she say to you, Charlie? You can tell me; it's alright.

CHARLIE: She didn't say anything.

RAY: You wouldn't lie to me, would you? Or conceal anything?

CHARLIE: No.

[*Pause.*]

RAY: Course you would, Charlie: you're an anthropologist. You believe people should—should—should live according to their culture. If Tony was knocked off for some ... some tribal reason, you'd hide it from me; am I right?

[*Pause.*]

CHARLIE: I—I—I—Ray ...

RAY: What about Kate? Is she safe?

[*Pause.*]

Charlie, you're not very convincing.

56

[CHARLIE *shuffles uncomfortably.*]

Alright. How do you feel about a charge of concealing a serious of-
fence?

CHARLIE: What?

RAY: I'm not joking.

CHARLIE: I know.

RAY: Because if you know something you're not telling, that's what you'll
get. Think about what it'll mean. Your grant money. The work you're
doing here. Think about it. I bend the law a hell of a lot so we can do
things tribal way. But if I turn a blind eye to this ... I might as well
not be here. Come on, Charlie: you know something. It's obvious.
You look like a fart on its way out.

[CHARLIE *laughs in spite of himself.*]

CHARLIE: Ray ... it's nothing.

RAY: In that case it can't hurt, can it?

CHARLIE: These people have just let me in.

RAY: I know. I know that, Charlie. It'll be okay; don't worry.

[*Pause.*]

CHARLIE: It ... It was the map.

RAY: The map?

CHARLIE: She—She met him at the waterhole. Kuninka Dreaming.

RAY: Tony? When?

CHARLIE: Sunday. He was guarding the ceremonial ground. All the
sacred objects ...

RAY: She see all that stuff?

CHARLIE: I think so.

RAY: Oh, shit. That was ... She didn't—They didn't ... ?

CHARLIE: I don't know. I don't know. I ... I ... Talk to Sarah. That's all
I found out.

RAY: Oh ... no point asking Sarah.

CHARLIE: Why not?

RAY: Because she wouldn't tell me. [*Calling*] Billy!

[BILLY *emerges from the house.* SARAH *follows.*]

We go have a talk with someone.

CHARLIE: Ray, it ... it doesn't mean ...

BILLY: Eh, boss.

RAY: What?

BILLY: More better this one been tribal way.

RAY: [*staring at him*] Let's go.

CHARLIE: Ray, for God's sake.

RAY: Come on, Billy.

[RAY *exits into the shadows.* BILLY *hesitates, looks at the others, then follows.*]

CHARLIE: Oh, fuck.

SARAH: Well ... exactly what did you expect?

[CHARLIE *turns.*]

CHARLIE: I ...

[*She goes inside.* CHARLIE *is left alone. He is suddenly aware he has been coolly observed by* POPPY. CHARLIE *can say nothing; rather he follows* SARAH *inside. Lights down on the doctor's house; lights up on* POPPY *by the campfire. He begins to sing. Climactic choral music. Lights up on the community advisor's living room, night. Outside,* RAY *enters and knocks.* DAVID *enters from inside the house. He answers the door.*]

DAVID: Oh. Hi. Come in.

[RAY *and* BILLY *enter.* DAVID *turns the music down.* POPPY *continues to sing.*]

I'm writing the sermon. Music always helps.

RAY: Sounds like you're really gunna clout 'em this week.

DAVID: Yes ... There's coffee made.

RAY: No, thanks.

[*Lights down on road.* RAY *picks up a brochure from* DAVID'*s table.*]

'Aboriginal and Torres Strait Islander Commission'. You looking for a job, mate?

DAVID: No, not really.

RAY: Thing is: I'm after some advice.

DAVID: Sure.

RAY: About Tony. I've been doing a bit of thinking in my quiet, plodding way.

DAVID: Mmm.

RAY: Might've come up with something.

DAVID: [*taking a seat*] Alright.

RAY: Remember how I said my instinct told me ... this whole thing wasn't right?

DAVID: Yep.

RAY: There's been no ... no crying or mourning over Tony's death.

DAVID: No. Well, he doesn't have relatives here. Just an uncle.

RAY: But it's unusual, isn't it? I would say it's unusual.

DAVID: Yeah ...

RAY: I mean, I've never seen a death ... ignored like this before. It bothered me. And then ... the body was very clean.

DAVID: Clean?

RAY: Yeah. I mean, he went out drinking, he was sitting in the dirt all night ... you know. Next morning he doesn't have a bit of dirt on him. What d'you think of that?

[DAVID *says nothing.*]

Well, I thought it was a bit weird. Then Sarah told me another weird thing: his feet are bruised.

DAVID: His feet?

RAY: Yeah. It's in her report. When you die the blood collects at the lowest part of the body. It makes a bruise. You don't always see it on a dark skin, but she said it was pretty clear. Now if he was lying down ... and had a heart attack ... why did the blood go to his feet?

DAVID: Well ... I don't ...

RAY: No, me neither, but then ... something came along which helped a bit: now, we know that ... Tony was having an affair ... with Kate.

DAVID: Was he?

RAY: No, Dave, I made it up. The point is: I just found out their last ... their last meeting happened at a spot where there's men's business going on. You know that?

DAVID: No. No, I didn't.

[BILLY *shifts uncomfortably.*]

RAY: No? Mmm. Well. Anyway. That sort of brought it into focus. So I've put these facts together into a theory. And I'd like your opinion.

DAVID: Is this confidential?

RAY: Absolutely.

DAVID: Alright.

RAY: My theory goes like this: Tony was killed for fucking his girlfriend on a sacred site. What d'you think?

[*Pause.*]

DAVID: It's, um ...

RAY: Let me spell it out a bit. He went out drinking with his mates, he drove home. Maybe someone drove him, I dunno. He was killed, the body was left in the car. The blood settled ... to his feet. They washed him ... in a ceremony while they sung his spirit out. And he was put in his bedroll so that Kate would find him in the morning ... and work out where she stands. And there's no mourning for him because ... well, because he broke a big sacred law. What d'you reckon? Does it hold water?

DAVID: No.

RAY: That's a shame: I was pleased with it.

DAVID: Ray ... he died of a heart attack. It's hard to see how you can make someone die of a heart attack.

RAY: Well ... there's a way of killing a man by ... [*Crooking his elbow.*] blocking both arteries in the neck. Maybe someone in the back seat. If you do it right there's a reflex stoppage of the heart.

DAVID: Nobody here could kill someone like that.

RAY: Ah, well, it's a lost art, isn't it? Maybe not quite lost.

DAVID: Poppy might say, 'Kudaitcha man'.

RAY: I bet he would. I bet he'd say all kinds of spooky stuff. But I don't believe in that. I think the old men commissioned a young bloke from around here. Strong physically, and really strong in his culture. Someone he knew. Course, most of the young blokes around here: they're out ... chasing girls or sniffing petrol. They don't have that secret law. But there's one ... that I can think of ... who might.

DAVID: Anything is possible, but ...

RAY: But how can I prove it? I don't think that'll be too hard. I just need to find someone who ... who saw it happen. Or heard about it.

DAVID: Like who?

RAY: Well ... you know: the washing, then carry the body around ... I mean all the way to Les and Kate's, for God sake. I thought: just about everybody must've known. Aboriginal people. You, for instance.

DAVID: I don't. I can't help.

RAY: Well, I'm curious to know, Dave ... how you knew there wasn't a mark on the body ... before he was examined.

DAVID: I ... Well, I just meant ... I couldn't see any marks.

RAY: It didn't sound like that. It sounded like you knew.

DAVID: Did it?

RAY: I put it to you this way: I'm giving you a chance. Like you gave me. You tell me if that little bastard is the one or I'll go to any of about a dozen people out there. Any one of whom will tell me if I want 'em to. And when they do I'll have you for concealing and you'll be fucked. Might even do time. Or have I got it wrong? Do you want to hang round here the rest of your life? [*Picking up the brochure*] ATSIC for you, wasn't it? Ladder up the public service? You better work out your priorities, boy.

DAVID: I don't ...

RAY: Don't what?

DAVID: Why are you doing this?

RAY: My job, Dave. Have to do my job. Don't I?

DAVID: You ...

> [RAY *laughs.*]

RAY: Well, let's put it this way: this dirty little hole is my Dreaming. Charlie should put it on his map: 'Ray's Dreaming'.

> [POPPY *redoubles his singing.*]

I am needed here. And that old bastard ... wants to get rid of me because I sent him down for shooting up his own Toyota. I mean: is that a joke?

DAVID: Poppy?

RAY: Who do you think? He's wants my blood. I can hear him singing now.

> [*He listens.*]

Can't you hear it?

> [DAVID *shakes his head.*]

It's him or me, Dave. Him or me. And if he ... instructed—if he *sanctioned* this killing ... I'm gunna make sure it's him. He's going away. And you're gunna help me.

DAVID: Ray ... I can't.

RAY: Then someone else will. And that'll be the end of your contribution to Aboriginal wealth and culture. So what's it to be? I'd like to let you off the hook but my hands are tied. I'm just doing a job, aren't I, Bill?

BILLY: You do it good, Ray.

RAY: [*to* DAVID] There you go. So come on: what d'you say?

DAVID: I thought we were friends.

RAY: We are.

> [*Outside,* POPPY *is joined by* MANNGA, TJULPU *and several other Aborigines.*]

DAVID: You're a prick.

RAY: That's a bit rugged from a man of the cloth, Dave. A pastor like yourself ... protecting a murderer. Don't you worry about that? I mean, what would God think? Doesn't really sit too well, does it?

DAVID: You—Don't you think I've thought of that?

RAY: Have you? Thought of what?

> [*Pause.*]

> Thought of what, Dave?

> [*Pause.*]

> Well, well.

DAVID: He did it.

RAY: What was that?

DAVID: He did it. Alright? Tjulpu killed him. It's tribal business; it's got nothing to do with you. Why don't you stay out of the whole fucking thing, maku yilykuwarra. [*'... witchetty grub. '*]

> [RAY *smiles.*]

RAY: Thanks, mate.

> [*Lights up on* POPPY*'s backyard, night.* POPPY, MANNGA, TJULPU *and several others sit around a fire.* POPPY *holds a half-finished dot painting which he discusses with* MANNGA. RAY *strides straight out of* DAVID*'s house into the midst of the group.* BILLY *follows at his hobbling pace. Lights down on* DAVID.]

[*To* TJULPU] You're in all sorts of shit, boy.

> [*The Aborigines stand warily.* RAY *takes out his handcuffs and slaps one end onto* TJULPU*'s left wrist.* TJULPU *pulls his arm away angrily.* RAY *hits him in the face and* TJULPU *falls like a log, dazed. A roar of protest goes up from the others, and people begin to enter from all sides.* MANNGA, *enraged, grabs his spear and adopts a fighting stance, only to find himself looking down the barrel of* RAY*'s pistol. The shouting dies as bystanders scamper out of the line of fire.* POPPY *grasps* MANNGA*'s spear-throwing wrist. He takes* MANNGA*'s spear.* RAY *keeps his eyes on* MANNGA.]

Billy!

BILLY: Yeh.

RAY: [*indicating* TJULPU] Put the cuffs on him.

> [BILLY *shifts uneasily.* RAY *becomes aware his order is not being carried out.*]

What?

BILLY: That one my tjampati.

RAY: [*sighting down the barrel at* MANNGA] He's your *what?*

BILLY: He's Tjangala, I'm Tjapaltjarri. I can't—I can't touch him boss.

RAY: You can't *touch* him?

BILLY: Wrong skin.

RAY: 'Wrong skin?' Billy ... that's not what I want to hear right now. [*Handing the pistol to* BILLY] Hold this.

[BILLY *holds the pistol awkwardly. As one, the bystanders move further back.* RAY *goes to* TJULPU, *who is recovering, turns him over roughly and puts the cuffs on his other wrist, then drags him up. He takes the gun from* BILLY. *Someone pushes* BILLY. BILLY *turns with a raised fist.*] Eh! Enough of that. Come on.

[RAY *drags* TJULPU *away. He holsters his gun, but keeps a hand on it. Lights down on* POPPY'*s backyard and lights up on the muster room of the police station and the road outside, night. The crowd follows, shouting and gesturing, as* RAY *directs* BILLY *and* TJULPU *into the muster room. The crowd hangs outside and continues to shout.* RAY *exits to the storage room and reappears with his shotgun. He loads it and stands at the front entrance.*]

[*Shouting*] What d'you want from me? Don't I look after you? Don't I take care of you? You'd sell me down, though, wouldn't you? [*Pointing at* POPPY] You think he look after you like me? He'll teach you to drive, will he? He keep the grog out? I built this place. I look after it.

[*The crowd is angry but a little uncertain: no one quite understands what* RAY *is talking about.*]

Well ... you treat me like watpalla I show you white law, don't you fuckin' worry. You want tribal way? I'll show you white law ...

[RAY *slams the door. The crowd hangs about.* GORDON *and* FARRELLY *enter at a distance.* FARRELLY *has the camera on his shoulder.*]

GORDON: What the fuck was that about?

FARRELLY: Who gives a fuck what it was about? It was fuckin' great!

[*Lights down on the road outside. Inside,* RAY *turns to face the handcuffed* TJULPU, *who stands, defiant, with* BILLY *nervously behind. Swinging the shotgun,* RAY *takes a couple of steps, eyes fixed on* TJULPU.]

RAY: You piece of shit.

BILLY: Boss ...

[RAY *doesn't move.*]
I put 'im lock-up. Okay?
RAY: I'm gunna —
BILLY: [*interrupting, grabbing the keys*] I put 'im lock-up now. He been settle down, eh? Okay.
[BILLY *opens the back door. Without looking at* TJULPU, BILLY *moves between* TJULPU *and* RAY. TJULPU *drops his eyes. In this manner* BILLY *manages to herd* TJULPU *off towards the back of the station. Lights up on the lock-up which is a separate building within the police compound.* RAY *watches abstractedly through the window as* BILLY *takes* TJULPU *to the lock-up. They reach the door and* TJULPU *will go no further.* BILLY *looks worriedly at* RAY, *then tentatively tries to push* TJULPU *through the door.* TJULPU *will not budge.* BILLY *is caught in an impossible dilemma. Clutching his shotgun,* RAY *stalks down to the lock-up.* TJULPU *prepares to stand his ground.* RAY *discharges the gun into the air and* TJULPU *is so stunned by the noise that he jumps halfway through the doorway.*]
RAY: Kumatjala, minipuka! [*'Come on, fucking cunt!'*]
[RAY *pushes him inside and slams the door. He glares at* BILLY, *then wanders back to the station.* BILLY *locks up and follows. A* GIRL *enters from behind the police compound and runs up to the crowd.*]
GIRL: He been lock-up! This way.
[*The crowd, including* GORDON *and* FARRELLY, *moves around the back of the compound and off.* TJULPU *catches a glimpse of them outside the compound. He shouts and waves, disturbed and frightened. From off, they shout back. Inside,* BILLY *re-enters. He puts the keys away.*]
BILLY: You do it good, Ray. No worries.
[RAY *looks at him, still clutching the shotgun.* BILLY *puts an arm around him.*]
[*Putting a hand on the shotgun*] You give me this one.
[RAY *pulls away from the embrace.*]
You give me beer.
RAY: Want a beer?
BILLY: Yeah.
RAY: Yeah, okay. I feel like one.

[RAY *sits with the shotgun between his knees.* BILLY *hesitates, then fetches two beers.* RAY *cracks his and takes a swig.* BILLY *stands watching, the unopened can in his hand.*]

Get some rest.

BILLY: [*lowering himself into a chair*] Oh ... I been wake-up too much. I been sit here little bit.

[RAY *watches him for a moment.*]

RAY: Okay ...

[RAY *takes another swig.* BILLY *watches him. Silence. Lights down on the police station and the lock-up. Lights up on the campfire, morning.* POPPY, MANNGA *and* DAVID *sit in conference. In the lock-up,* TJULPU *sings to himself.*]

DAVID: [*crossing his wrists, to* POPPY] Ray wants to put you in gaol. Because of that kumunjayi teacher one.

POPPY: Mmm.

DAVID: I think you should go for a while. Maybe stay with your nephew Kiwirrkurra. [*Crossing his wrists*] Otherwise I think you might go this one Alice Springs.

POPPY: [*indicating* MANNGA] His grandson: you help 'im, eh?

DAVID: Yeah, I do what I can. I write letter. I talk up for him in Alice Springs, okay?

MANNGA: Wiya. You: get that one now.

[DAVID *looks from one to the other.*]

DAVID: I can't.

MANNGA: You get Tjulpu now.

POPPY: [*to* DAVID] You hear? He sing himself.

DAVID: I don't—I can't. I just can't.

POPPY: You: blackpalla, watpalla?

[DAVID *stares at them helplessly.*]

You go. You go, watpalla.

DAVID: Poppy —

POPPY: [*interrupting*] I stay. Politpalla go! You no write letter, no talk Alice Springs. That watpalla way.

DAVID: Poppy, I do some things watpalla way. I have to. Watpallas are strong: they give us everything for Wala Wala: food, drink, petrol, houses. Everything. I want to make us strong like that. But I have to do it watpalla way.

POPPY: Wiya. [*Picking up a handful of dirt*] My country. Watpalla not give me this one. *You* tell constable Tjulpu finish that kumunjayi. You go, watpalla.

DAVID: What ... ? What d'you want me to do?

MANNGA: You get Tjulpu now.

POPPY: [*to* DAVID] He sing, that one; he die pretty soon.

DAVID: How? How can we get him?

[POPPY *and* MANNGA *glance at one another.* MANNGA *produces a heavy noose.* DAVID *takes the noose gingerly, letting it lie in his hands. He looks at the others, confused.*]

POPPY: You: blackpalla, watpalla?

[*Lights up in the muster room, morning. Lights down on the camp-fire. The electric guitar starts up, off.* BILLY *is asleep in his chair.* TJULPU *continues to sing, now cross-legged in his cell.* GORDON *and* FARRELLY *look hopefully at* RAY.]

RAY: No, forget it.

GORDON: Come on, Ray. We've got a deadline. We've got Poppy on tape. We need your version.

RAY: Poppy?

GORDON: We're try'n'a get both sides, you know.

RAY: What'd he say?

GORDON: He made a statement. A sort of ... his own version of events.

RAY: Is that right?

GORDON: Great stuff. Lots of colour. He made you out as a colourful character.

RAY: Did he just?

[*Pause.*]

What about David? He talk to you?

GORDON: No ...

RAY: Alright. Yeah, alright, let's do it. Eh, Billy!

[BILLY *starts awake and looks around.*]

Get me a coffee, will you?

[BILLY *rubs his eyes and slouches off to the kitchen. As* FARRELLY *sets up the camera* RAY *takes a comb from his pocket and puts his hair in order with a few strokes. During the following* BILLY *takes a drink and a sandwich to* TJULPU *in the lock-up. They avoid eye contact:* BILLY *leaves the food just inside the door but* TJULPU *doesn't touch it.*]

RAY: [*to* GORDON] This gunna be six-o'clock news, or what?

66

GORDON: Yeah, for the moment. Might wind up a special in the end. We're getting all sorts of footage.

FARRELLY: [*putting the camera on his shoulder*] Yep.

GORDON: Noddies first, eh? [*To* RAY] We'll just be a second.

RAY: Uh huh.

[FARRELLY *moves to get an angle on* GORDON *looking at* RAY.]

GORDON: [*to* FARRELLY] Okay?

FARRELLY: Rolling.

[GORDON *looks at* RAY, *nods, cocks his head to one side, looks thoughtful, looks serious.*]

GORDON: [*to* RAY] Tjulpu Tjangala has spent almost his entire life in the desert; how much contact has he had with white people?

RAY: Well, it ... it wouldn't be —

GORDON: [*interrupting, to* FARRELLY] Cut.

[FARRELLY *repositions to get a shot of* RAY.]

[*To* RAY] Okay, don't go any further. Just hang on to that answer. Those were just reactions to what you're gunna tell me. We cut them in later.

RAY: You do them now?

GORDON: Ahhh ... not always.

FARRELLY: Yep.

GORDON: Okay.

FARRELLY: Rolling.

GORDON: [*to the microphone*] Tjulpu has spent his entire life in the desert; how much contact do you think he's had with white people?

RAY: I'm not sure.

GORDON: It's not much, though, is it?

RAY: No.

GORDON: In fact he doesn't even speak English, does he?

RAY: No, he's a traditional Pintupi speaker.

GORDON: So it's possible he's being held under a law he's never heard of. Do you think that's fair?

RAY: Well, that ... that's not for me to decide. We're ... The police ... um, are obliged to treat everyone equally.

GORDON: Equal ... but not fair.

[*Pause.*]

Although Mr Tjangala's had no contact with white law, his father was not so lucky: he died in police custody. In fact, in your custody.

RAY: Yes. Yes, that's right.

GORDON: Would you say he received equal treatment?

RAY: Yes. He did.

GORDON: It's Aboriginal custom to avoid places where ... where death has occurred. Where family have died. But Tjulpu is now being held in the same cell his own father died in a few months ago. How do you think he feels right now?

RAY: He would ... It's not—It's unfortunate but it's the only cell we have.

GORDON: Isn't it possible he might kill himself?

RAY: No, that would be ...

GORDON: Just as his father did? Maybe you'd call that 'equal treatment'?

RAY: Listen, that had nothing to do with me, mate.

[*Pause.*]

GORDON: Why are you still here?

RAY: I ... We did everything we could.

GORDON: But he still died.

[RAY *searches for an answer. Long pause.*]

Cut. Thanks, Ray.

[GORDON *and* FARRELLY *pack up wordlessly. Lights up on the road outside the police station, day.* FARRELLY *leaves with the camera. As* GORDON *heads for the door* RAY *takes his arm.*]

RAY: [*to* FARRELLY] Won't be a tick. Just want a word.

[RAY *closes the door, stranding* FARRELLY *and the Betacam outside. He drags* GORDON *back into the room.*]

[*To* GORDON] Been doing this long, have you? Sniffing out shit for a living?

GORDON: What's your problem, Ray?

[*Pause.*]

RAY: I been a copper seventeen years. My dad was a copper. You know, in the old days, if the blackfellas killed a bloke they weren't meant to ... they'd dig a hole in a termite mound, put the body in. Few hours the termites'd fix up the hole, body would never be found.

[RAY *releases him.*]

GORDON: What's that supposed to mean?

RAY: It means there's a lot of termites in the desert.

[*The telephone rings.* RAY *stares at him.* GORDON *backs to the door and joins* FARRELLY *outside. They exit.* RAY *answers the phone.*]

Police ... Superintendent ... Yes, sir: a plane, if that's ... ? Sir ... it's ... it's a bit urgent ...

[BILLY *enters with a cup of coffee.*]

Well ... where's the search area? They could drop in on the way back; it'd be only ... only a couple of hours out of the ... No. There's no trouble at all. No. Sir ... you'll call me when the plane is—is—is available ... Yes, sir. Right. Thanks.

[RAY *slams down the handset.*]

Fuck. No fuckin' plane!

[*Pause.*]

BILLY: You want coffee?

RAY: Yeah. Thanks, mate.

[*He takes the cup from* BILLY *and swigs it. Outside,* DAVID *heads towards the police compound.*]

Okay. You fell asleep: you can watch him for a bit. Be careful, alright?

BILLY: Yuwa.

RAY: I go rest. I come back later.

BILLY: Okay, Ray.

[RAY *leaves and runs into* DAVID *outside. Lights down on the station.*]

RAY: What d'you want?

DAVID: [*nodding towards the back*] Talk to the prisoner.

RAY: Oh, him. Think you'll convert him?

DAVID: You'd be surprised.

RAY: I hear in Balgo every year they dance the Stations of the Cross. They really get into the taunting. That's their favourite bit, the taunting.

DAVID: I want to tell him what's going on. I've rung Legal Aid.

RAY: Okay.

DAVID: How long is he here for?

RAY: Don't know. Day or two. Soon as they can send a plane.

DAVID: Right. You look like shit, by the way.

RAY: Least I'm not the same colour.

[*They grin at one another.*]

[*Calling*] Billy! [*To* DAVID] I'll get some sleep.

[BILLY *comes out as* RAY *exits.* DAVID *looks at* BILLY, *and they head out the back. Lights crossfade from the road to the lock-up, day.* TJULPU *stands as he sees* DAVID. *Lights down on the lock-up. Lights up on the bedroom of the school teacher's house, day.* KATE *looks out the window as* LES *puts on a fresh shirt.* KATE *is wearing her nightdress.*]

LES: Stop that, please.

[KATE *continues to stare out.*]

Will you stop it!

[KATE *looks at him a moment, then turns back to the window.*]

KATE: We're frauds.

LES: Nonsense.

KATE: We're frauds.

LES: So hot today.

[*Pause.*]

I don't understand how you can say that. Just because no one came to school this morning. Quite frankly I find it insulting to Tony's memory. He certainly believed in what we're doing. Tony was an example ... of—He would've made ... something of himself, I'm sure. He would've ... I find it most sad that ... that the best and brightest are so often the ones we lose.

[*He finishes putting on his shirt and checks his appearance in the mirror.*]

There we are. Face the world.

[*He goes to* KATE *and touches her.*]

There's no one out there.

KATE: I can—I can feel ...

LES: No, no. There's no one there. [*Going back to the mirror*] It's important, though, we shouldn't waver. That's why I taught an empty classroom: to make a point. They'll be back. As long as we stand firm. Tony would've wanted us to —

KATE: [*interrupting*] How can you say what Tony would've wanted?

LES: I beg your pardon.

KATE: You didn't know Tony, what he thought, what ... what he could do.

LES: I think I knew him a little better than you.

KATE: Why? Did you fuck him?

[LES *is struck dumb.* KATE *turns back to the window.*]

LES: I don't know you. I don't know you at all.

KATE: No.

LES: What makes you think you can speak to me in that fashion?

KATE: I don't know! Something's wrong with me, can't you see?

LES: It certainly is. It certainly is; these ideas of yours —

KATE: [*interrupting*] Do you want me to tell you what it was like? Do you want a description?

[*He looks at her.*]

LES: No. No, that won't be necessary. I imagine ... I imagine ... you were in love with him, were you? It was love, was it?

KATE: No.

LES: Not love?

KATE: No.

LES: Lust, then.

KATE: I don't know. Yes. I don't know. Les ... something ... that he had, some ... knowledge ... that he had; Les ... I've seen the place where ... little boys are killed ... and made into men.

[LES *looks at her, disturbed.*]

That's why we have to go: I've seen things, and—and people here ... are aware of what I've seen. I think ... I think —

LES: [*interrupting*] No, no.

KATE: Les —

LES: [*interrupting*] No, no, no, we won't go. I won't let you do this.

[KATE *stares at him.*]

I love it here. I love these people, I love what we're doing, I love this land, I love everything about it. This is home for me. I won't give it up; do you hear me?

KATE: [*screaming*] I hate it here! I hate it! I hate these dirty, dumpy little places. I hate their ugliness. I hate these people, I hate ... touching them. I hate their smell. I hate their hands and their ... fetid breath. They're ugly, dirty black animals. They're boongs. Coons. Niggers. They should be rounded up and shot; they should be exterminated. They should be ... hunted like ...

[LES *stares at her.*]

Oh, God ... [*Reaching out to him*] Les ...

[*He pulls away. He looks at his watch.*]

LES: I have a class.

[*He goes to the door.*]

I think, under the circumstances, we'll tough it out, don't you?

[*He exits towards the school.* KATE *stares after him, then goes into the house. Lights crossfade to the station, afternoon.* TJULPU *is no longer singing. The football is on the television: the Tigers are playing.* BILLY *enters with a beer. He hesitates a moment when*

he thinks someone might be at the door, then realises he's safe.
With immense satisfaction he settles down in front of the footy.
The phone rings. BILLY *reaches out and picks it up.*]

BILLY: Yuwa ... He not here. Been sleeping ... Yuwa, he been lock-up.

[*Lights up on the lock-up.* TJULPU *has attached a length of rope*
to the ceiling. The end is tied into a noose.]

He been finish 'im. Tony Mackay. Trainee teacher ... Yuwa. I tell 'im:
Kerry Thompson ... *Kidney Morning Herald.*

[BILLY *hangs up and continues to watch the footy. He looks up in*
time to see TJULPU *attach the noose to the top of the cell.*]

[*Calling*] Eh! Eh, you! You wait! Wait on!

[TJULPU *glances at him.* BILLY *jumps up and hobbles out the back*
as TJULPU *hauls himself up the noose and inserts his head.* BILLY
is inhibited by the skins taboo. He begins to panic. He shuffles off
towards RAY's *house.*]

Boss! Eh, boss! Ray!

[*As soon as he is gone the* FIRST MAN *and* SECOND MAN *run*
on with several others. Someone cuts the lock with bolt cutters,
another cuts the rope and TJULPU *starts to gasp and cough. The*
FIRST *and* SECOND MAN *spirit him away. Several others follow and*
walk over their tracks. RAY *runs on, still in his rumpled uniform*
and half asleep. He catches sight of a few people wandering off,
having obliterated the trace. Then RAY *sees the empty lock-up.*
He runs inside and examines the end of the rope. BILLY *follows*
him on as fast as he can, then slows his pace when he sees what's
happened. He looks for tracks on the ground and realises it's
hopeless. He goes to RAY *in the lock-up.*]

He been hangin' ... Boss ...

[RAY *lashes out with his fist and knocks* BILLY *to the ground.*]

RAY: You fuckin' idiot! You fuckin' ... fuckin' idiot.

[BILLY *stares at him miserably.* RAY *storms out, slams the door*
and heads for the station. Lights down on the lock-up and the
muster room of the police station. Lights up on a cleared area
away from the community, day. DAVID *and* POPPY *sit waiting. Off,*
a car drives up. The doors open and close, and it drives off again.
POPPY *and* DAVID *stand as* MANNGA *and* TJULPU *enter.* TJULPU
is now in traditional dress with digging stick and two hunting
spears. MANNGA *also carries a spear.*]

72

POPPY: [*to* TJULPU] Nyuntupa tjamulu nyuntunya yantayantanu. [*'Your grandad looks after you, eh?'*]

TJULPU: Yuwa. Ngayunya tjukutiukunguru. [*'Since I was little.'*] [*Miming bars*] Nguyulu wiyana pulkara mingkuringu ngurra palaku. [*'I didn't like that place much.'*]

DAVID: No. Not a good place.

TJULPU: Malpu yutulu. [*'Too many ghosts.'*]

POPPY: Mmm, ghost. Too much.

TJULPU: [*to* DAVID] Nganana malaku yanku ngayku ngurrarakutu. [*'We'll go back to my country.'*]

DAVID: Yuwa. You go back.

POPPY: You too.

DAVID: Me?

POPPY: Yuwa. [*Indicating* TJULPU] You drive this one; he teach you, eh? You go, go, come back: you get one head band, eh?

DAVID: No, Poppy, I'm Lutheran. Initiation: that's not for me.

POPPY: Eh, you go, more better. [*Crossing his wrists*] Politpalla put you this one. Take you Alice Springs.

DAVID: No, I'll be okay.

POPPY: [*indicating* TJULPU] You help this one; [*Crossing his wrists*] they put you this one.

DAVID: They don't know I help him.

POPPY: Someone tell 'em.

DAVID: Someone tell them?

POPPY: Yuwa.

DAVID: Who?

POPPY: Someone. You go.

DAVID: Poppy, I can't live in the desert. I've been sitting down too long. I've got too much watpalla in me; I eat their food, I do everything watpalla way. I'll die out there.

[POPPY *picks up a stick and draws concentric circles in the dirt.*]

POPPY: [*indicating the circles*] This one our camp. You little one, you sleep here.

[POPPY *draws another group of concentric circles at a point further off.*]

That one watpalla camp. [*Crossing to a point midway between*] You been put your camp here.

[DAVID *shakes his head to himself.* POPPY *takes* MANNGA's *spear and draws a line between the two camps.*]

We waiting, waiting, waiting, you don't come back. [*Crossing back to his circle, indicating* TJULPU] This one teach you how to put your camp back here. You go.

[POPPY *places* MANNGA's *spear in* DAVID's *hands.* DAVID *handles it awkwardly.*]

DAVID: Poppy ...

POPPY: You: watpalla, blackpalla?

DAVID: I'll die out there.

[POPPY *crosses to the mid-point line and obliterates it.*]

POPPY: No middle road.

[DAVID *stares at him. Lights down on the cleared area and up on the kitchen and living room of the doctor's house, morning. A blustery wind blows around the house.* CHARLIE *sips a cup of coffee as he carefully marks a trail on his Dreaming map. Off, a car starts and drives away.* SARAH *enters the kitchen.*]

CHARLIE: Who was that?

SARAH: Andrew's car, I think.

CHARLIE: Mmm. He was taking me out tomorrow. On a maintenance ceremony.

SARAH: Where are they all going?

CHARLIE: I dunno. Away.

[*Pause.*]

Fuck it. Fuck, fuck, fuck!

SARAH: Come on, sweetheart.

CHARLIE: Oh, what?

[*Pause.*]

The *fucking* cops. I can't believe it.

SARAH: Yes, alright.

CHARLIE: I've worked hard on this.

SARAH: Yes.

CHARLIE: So ... *close*, I was ...

[*He stares at the Dreaming map, then tears it down.*]

SARAH: Charlie!

[*She picks up the map, sits and tries to smooth it out.*]

Will you stop it? You're being ridiculous. [*Fingering a tear*] Oh, look.

[*She starts to fold the map.* CHARLIE *stares at her.*]

CHARLIE: I've just missed out ... on the most important part of my original research.

SARAH: Yes.

CHARLIE: What's ridiculous about it?

SARAH: Nothing.

CHARLIE: What? What? Why am I ridiculous?

SARAH: You're not. I'm sorry.

[CHARLIE *turns away. Pause.*]

CHARLIE: [*savagely*] Fuck!

SARAH: Stop it! Now look, I've had enough of this. You've been stamping round the house all day like a ... an angry schoolboy and I'm sick of it.

CHARLIE: Just shut up! Shut ... up!

SARAH: No. Now I'm sorry for your work but throwing your arms about won't help.

CHARLIE: Thank you, what ... very sound advice, I'm sure.

SARAH: For goodness' sake.

[CHARLIE *raises his arm to hit her.* SARAH *flinches and holds up her hands.* CHARLIE *holds the posture for a moment, then turns and paces around the room.* SARAH *lowers her hands and looks at him angrily.*]

CHARLIE: What is wrong with you?

SARAH: What's wrong with you?

CHARLIE: Nothing two years' research wouldn't fix.

SARAH: Why do I get the feeling you're acting? I get it a lot from you.

CHARLIE: I don't know. I don't know what goes on in your head.

SARAH: I don't imagine you do. Why don't you *do* something, Charlie? If you did something I might take you more seriously.

CHARLIE: Like what?

[*Pause.*]

SARAH: Well ... why didn't you hit me?

CHARLIE: What?

SARAH: Why didn't you hit me? Come on, Charlie: I'm being a bitch.

CHARLIE: You're being ridiculous.

SARAH: You're saying that because I just said it to you. Why can't you do something original?

CHARLIE: What d'you want me to do? Smash the table?

SARAH: No: that would be petulant.

CHARLIE: Then *what?*

SARAH: I don't know. Something I can't guess in advance.

[*Pause.*]

CHARLIE: I'm going to back Sydney.

SARAH: Oh.

CHARLIE: I got a letter from Margaret. There's a lectureship going at New South.

[*Pause.*]

SARAH: That was unexpected.

CHARLIE: Yeah.

SARAH: You're going back to her.

CHARLIE: I'm not doing anything; my ... my work is fucked and ... money doesn't grow on trees, and ... so on.

[SARAH *stares at the map for a moment, then begins to cry.*] Oh, shit.

[*He goes to sit next to her but she slaps his hand away.*]

SARAH: Get away.

[*He watches helplessly.*]

CHARLIE: I can't hang round here ...

SARAH: I didn't think you would. I thought ... we—we—we might hang round somewhere else together.

[CHARLIE *turns and stares out the window.*]

SARAH: You're not a real person, are you? You're a fake, a sort of ... I don't know ... human ... lecture tour of the dead heart.

[*She breaks down into sobs again.* CHARLIE *goes to her.*]

CHARLIE: [*touching her shoulders*] Sarah —

SARAH: [*interrupting, slapping him away*] No! Don't touch me, so stupid, so *stupid*, I do it every time.

CHARLIE: What d'you expect? I never said I was—I was ... we were ... some ... item, for life.

SARAH: Oh, shut up! I'm—I'm sick of it. I'm sick of listening to you; I don't even *like* you anymore. I thought ... I thought we were ... the same ... sort of person; I thought we were ... here looking for something. I thought you were *brave*, that's what I thought. I thought you came out here because you were brave, but you're a coward. You know the man I respect out here? The one white man? Can you guess?

[*Pause.*]

CHARLIE: Ray?

SARAH: That's right. That's right; do you know why?

CHARLIE: I'm sure you'll tell me.

SARAH: Because he does what he believes in. He doesn't care if a hundred people want to stop him. He wouldn't care if it was two hundred. He doesn't count the cost. I think ... he's a very powerful man.

CHARLIE: He's a lunatic.

SARAH: You don't understand me, do you?

CHARLIE: Of course I do.

SARAH: I don't think so. I don't think so. Otherwise you'd know how to *do* things; you'd know how to ... You don't *believe anything*, Charlie. In the rightness of anything. That's what it is. You don't *believe* in what you're doing; you're just so .. so ... so ... *much* like my husband.

[CHARLIE *stares at her, then picks up his damaged map and folds it carefully. Lights down on the living room. Lights up on Wala Wala, day.* GORDON *stares earnestly into* FARRELLY's *camera.*]

GORDON: For over six hours now an exodus has been in progress as the population of Wala Wala scatters itself among other settlements in the area, or in some cases perhaps into the desert itself. Yesterday afternoon a dozen police converged on the tiny settlement when a suspect, detained for questioning over the death of a twenty-five-year-old Aboriginal man ... escaped from the police station. Police have since viewed footage taken by this reporter of an angry mob surrounding the police station the day before. In the meantime, as the police move in, the Aborigines are moving out. The future for those remaining in this tiny community ... is uncertain. This is Gordon Reynolds, on location for the Seven Network.

[*Pause.*]

Cut. 'Exodus' is too much, isn't it? 'Flight', maybe.

FARRELLY: Yep.

GORDON: 'The community is in flight —' No ... sounds like Qantas.

[*Lights down on Wala Wala; lights up on the office of the police station, day.* SENIOR SERGEANT WARREN OAKS, CIB, *sits with his feet up on* RAY's *desk thumbing through a copy of the* Centralian Advocate. RAY *himself stands to one side.*]

OAKS: Yes ... Not really ... ideal. Seen this?

RAY: What?

OAKS: [*handing over the paper*] Your bloke. Tjulpu Thingamy. Page three.

[RAY *glances at the story.*]

77

RAY: Um ... sir ... about the search ...

OAKS: I can't see the need for it, constable.

RAY: Why not?

OAKS: Because there's no evidence. You need evidence to convict a felon and I have yet to see any.

RAY: But ... there's David Muller, community adviser.

OAKS: I don't see any signed statements.

RAY: No, sir ... [*'but ...'*]

OAKS: I know that you blokes in uniform don't think much of us at CIB, but you might have called us. We're not complete fuckwits. We do know how to get a statement from a witness which is more than you, apparently. Now ... I have been here only a short time, but I have obtained a statement from the doctor here and her diagnosis is that your Mr McKay died of a heart attack.

[RAY *snorts.*]

Is that funny?

RAY: But, sir ...

OAKS: Have a medical degree as well, do you, constable?

[*Pause.*]

I've put a bulletin out for Mr Muller and Mr Tjangala to say they're wanted for questioning; in the meantime that body is going back to Alice, and if the Coroner tells me there's no evidence he was killed, then as far as I'm concerned, he wasn't.

RAY: Sir ... the blacks have a way of killing people that ... that doesn't ... *leave* any marks.

OAKS: Do they? How interesting. I'm sure a jury will race to convict on that piece of testimony.

RAY: One interview would get it out of him. Tjulpu. He doesn't know anything about white law: a bit of pressure and he'd tell us.

OAKS: You better pray he does.

RAY: That's why we have to do a search.

OAKS: Chances are they'll turn up at another settlement.

RAY: David will. But Tjulpu won't.

OAKS: Chances are he will.

RAY: He spent his whole life in the desert; he won't join another settlement.

OAKS: Constable, you're telling me fairy stories. Nobody lives in the desert any more.

RAY: There aren't many left, but —

OAKS: [*interrupting*] There are none.

RAY: Sir —

OAKS: [*interrupting*] Constable ... I think you've done enough, don't you?
[*They stare at one another.*]

BILLY: [*from outside, calling*] Ray ...
[*Lights up on the lock-up, day.* BILLY *sits huddled on the concrete floor.*]
[*Calling*] Ray?

OAKS: Who's that?

RAY: Billy Curlew, sir.

OAKS: The blacktracker?

RAY: Sir.

OAKS: What the fuck is he doing in the lock-up?

RAY: Teach him to pay attention.
[OAKS *stares at him.*]

OAKS: The man is not a dog, Constable.

BILLY: [*calling*] Please, boss ...

RAY: No, sir. Dogs are smarter.
[OAKS *stares, then steps close to* RAY.]

OAKS: Listen, you dirty little tyrant, you don't make the rules out here.
This is not your private fiefdom. You think it is, don't you? You
think you know better than the poor plodding coppers back at head
office, following all those pedantic little rules and regulations that
big men like you really can't be bothered with. Let me tell you,
the rule book is there for a purpose. It keeps us all out of trouble,
and when you chuck it on the shit heap in the end you always wind
up under it. And believe me, that's where you're going. A mate of
mine tells me Internal Affairs is looking at you right now and you
have no chance of staying here. In fact, on current form I'd say you
don't have much chance of staying in the Force. Understand? That
story—That ... interview ... on television made you look like a nut
case. A vicious little thug who likes bumping off the odd boong.
The local papers are berserk; *I* ... have been fielding questions from
the *Sydney Morning Bloody Herald*, for God sake. I'm sure by the
weekend we'll be a mini series.
[OAKS *stares at him.*]
They're going to throw you to the lions, mate. And I think it's no
more than you deserve.

[OAKS *opens the desk drawer and removes the keys for the lock-up.*]
Now. Release that man. I have to do an interview with your Mr Reynolds, try and clean up this mess. Fortunately I am on good terms with Mr Reynolds. You can have your office back.
[OAKS *leaves the office and exits.* RAY *stares at the keys in his hand, then looks out at* BILLY. RAY *goes into the office and re-enters with his shotgun. He goes to the lock-up and opens the door.* BILLY *stares up at him.*]

BILLY: Ray?

[*Pause.*]

I didn't mean to let 'im go. I mean to keep 'im, but he was ... he was hangin', boss. He was hangin' up like other one; I don't *like* that one. I don't *like* it ... Boss?

RAY: [*gesturing at him with the shotgun*] Couldn't keep your fuckin' trap shut, could you? Couldn't just ...

BILLY: I seen 'im, Ray. I seen his ghost in here. I think ... he been comin' for me, Ray. He been comin'.

[RAY *looks up around the lock-up. He takes a few steps back.*]

RAY: No, he's not. No, Billy Boy. He's dead and fuckin' gone. You put your mind at rest. I'm on the job; I'll get those fuckin' bastards and ... things'll be right again.

[RAY *turns and, clutching his shotgun, runs off.* BILLY *hesitantly emerges from the lock-up. He tries to smooth his rumpled uniform without success.*]

BILLY: He don't like me no more. He don't like me. He don't like me no more.

[*Lights down on the lock-up. Lights up on the spinifex fire, night.* POPPY *is seated with the* FIRST *and* SECOND MAN. *Each has cards in his hands.*]

SECOND MAN: That constable, he wild, eh?

POPPY: He take one Toyota, go.

FIRST MAN: He chase 'em, that politpalla?

SECOND MAN: Cheeky bugger.

POPPY: That one David, that one Tjulpu, go ... go ... They driving long road, driving long desert ... Finish. No road; Toyota finish.

FIRST MAN: They bog that one.

POPPY: Yuwa. They walking. Politpalla track 'em, driving, driving ... Tjulpu, David, walking, walking ...

[*Lights down on the fire. Lights up on a rocky outcrop, late after-noon.* TJULPU *enters with a clump of spinifex tied with hair string to the shorter of his two spears. He also carries two feathered pieces of emu skin. He pulls some debris away, then pushes spear and spinifex down a crevice in the rock. About a metre disap-pears. He waits a moment, then draws the spear rapidly back. Like a plunger it forces water up before it, which pours into a little reservoir* TJULPU *has dug in the earth.* TJULPU *drinks from it.* DAVID *staggers on, exhausted. He drops gratefully into a sit-ting position.* TJULPU *looks at him, cups a little more water in his hand and drinks.* DAVID *watches him for a moment before he realises.*]

DAVID: Oh, shit.

[TJULPU *grins broadly as* DAVID *crawls over to the water and sucks up a few drops.*]

Piruku kutjupa kalya ngukulku? [*'Any more water to drink?'*]

TJULPU: Yuwa.

[TJULPU *once more puts his spear down the crevice and brings up a little water into* DAVID's *cupped hands.* DAVID *drinks greedily.* TJULPU *gives* DAVID *mulbo, a fungus which is acceptable bush food.*]

TJULPU: Nganana ngayuku ngurrangka ngaraku kuwarri. Ngaangka nguranyi mulbo nga mingkulpa kanga ngayuku ngurrara tjakipirri. Ngayupa wiya mungukutjirratjarrku. [*'We'll be in my country soon. Here there's only mulbo and mingkulpa but in my country there's emu and euro. We won't be hungry then.'*]

DAVID: Yaaltji tiwa? [*'How far?'*]

TJULPU: [*pointing*] Tjintu palawana. [*'A day that way.'*]

[TJULPU *settles down to work on the two pieces of feathered skin.*]

DAVID: A day? Oh, God. I feel sick.

TJULPU: Walpa pitjangu. [*'Wind is coming.'*]

DAVID: 'Wind'? Big wind?

TJULPU: Yuwa ngayuku kutalu, palunya pitjala kirruganlku nganapa tjamana mungawinki. [*'Yeah, my brother. He'll come and cover our tracks tomorrow.'*] [*Pointing to* DAVID's *shoes*] Yuwani ngayunya ngaanya. [*'Give me those.'*]

DAVID: These?

TJULPU: Yuwa.

DAVID: No, I need them. Ngayuku tjamana nyunnga. Wiya nyuntupa pirinypa. [*'My feet are soft. Not like yours.'*]

TJULPU: [*holding up the feathered skins*] Ngayulu nyuntunya ngaanya kutjunatana yungku. [*'I'll give you these instead.'*] More better.

DAVID: 'More better', eh?

TJULPU: Nyuntu puya pirinypa yanku ngaaku. [*'You'll walk like smoke in these.'*]

DAVID: I'll walk like smoke.

[DAVID *begins to take off his shoes, then stops.*]

They're no good for my feet. I won't get a hundred yards.

TJULPU: Tjana wiya mitulku nyuntunya ngaangka. [*'They won't track you in these.'*]

DAVID: No one's coming after us. Tjana wiya watiwatilku. [*'They won't bother.'*] They just wait for us ... wait till we turn up.

TJULPU: [*pointing into the distance*] Ngawa ngarranya. [*'Look there.'*]

[DAVID *looks into the distance and finally makes out something.*]

To-yo-ta.

DAVID: Yuwa. They must've seen the car.

TJULPU: Tjana nyangunya mutikayi. Tjana ngurrinyi nganapa. [*'They've seen that Toyota. They're looking for us.'*] [*Taking hold of his shoes*] Yuwani ngayunya ngaanya puta walalu. [*'Give me those shoes now, quickly.'*]

[DAVID *allows* TJULPU *to remove his shoes and socks.* TJULPU *takes hold of each of* DAVID'*s big toes and dislocates them.* DAVID *yells and holds his feet.*]

Nyuntupa tjamanalu nyanku tjaatu yankukitjalu. [*'Your feet will see where to go.'*]

DAVID: Oh, shit ...

[TJULPU *carefully ties the emu skin shoes onto* DAVID'*s feet.*]

TJULPU: [*pointing towards his country*] Nyuntu yarra palawana. Ngayulu ngurringkuna nyuntupa ngula. [*'You go that way. I'll find you later.'*]

DAVID: Split up?

TJULPU: [*pulling on* DAVID'*s shoes*] Ngayulu tjamana paltjulpa wanti-katiku walpalalu. [*'I'll set a trail for the watpallas.'*]

[TJULPU *stands to go. The shoes feel very strange and he laughs.*]

DAVID: I can't walk like this; I'll die out there. Ngayulu wiyana yanku ngayulu wiyanatju waltjalu yantayantanlku ngaaku. [*'I can't walk. I can't look after myself out here.'*]

TJULPU: Nyuntupa mamatura kuru nyuntupa tjamnaku. Nyuntu yanku puyu pirinypa, nyuntunu nyaku. Ngayulu nyuntunya ngampurrmanku. Wiya yurru kulintjaku. [*'Your toes are eyes for your feet. You'll walk like smoke, you'll see. I look after you. Don't worry.'*] [*Pointing*] Nyuntu yanku tali palakutu. Kurranyku mungarriku ngaanya. Ngayulu ngurrikunaku nyuntupa mungawinki. [*'You go to those hills. It'll be dark soon. I'll find you in the morning.'*]

[TJULPU *exits.* DAVID *stands carefully and grimaces.*]

DAVID: [*to himself*] My toes are eyes for my feet. God, help me.

[*Very gingerly he hobbles off according to* TJULPU*'s directions. Lights down on the rocky outcrop and up on the desert.* TJULPU *enters, still wearing* DAVID*'s shoes. He stops, takes off the shoes and carries them as he walks carefully backwards the way he's come. Lights up on* POPPY*'s campfire, the* FIRST *and* SECOND MAN *in attendance.*]

FIRST MAN: He put trail for that politpalla, eh?

[TJULPU *exits, walking backwards. Lights crossfade to dusk. A stiff wind is blowing.* RAY *enters, carrying his shotgun and a water bottle. He follows* TJULPU*'s two sets of tracks to the point at which they stop. He is mystified. He looks back, then at the surrounding desert.*]

RAY: [*shouting*] Fuck!

[*Lights down on the desert. At the spinifex fire the* FIRST *and* SECOND MAN *fall about laughing. Wind.*]

POPPY: Now ... big wind come!

SECOND MAN: [*jumping up*] Eh! Tjulpu's brother, that wind.

POPPY: Yuwa.

[*The* SECOND MAN *exits. Howling wind. Lights down on the spinifex fire; lights up on the desert, night.* RAY *enters with a powerful torch, his shotgun and an HF radio strapped to his back. A cloth is wrapped around his nose and mouth against the sand. He stumbles across a trailing rope. He examines it, tugs it, begins to follow its length.*]

RAY: Hey! Hey! Hello?

[*The rope leads him to a figure.* RAY *directs the beam of his torch to reveal a noose around the neck of the* SECOND MAN, *now dressed in check shirt and jeans.* RAY *drops the rope and raises his shotgun.*]

Danny? Danny, what ... ?

[RAY *is cut off as the* SECOND MAN *cries out, then begins to dance.*
POPPY *can be heard, singing.*]

Hey. Cut it out.

[*The* SECOND MAN *laughs and continues dancing.* RAY *pulls the
cloth away from his face and stares at him for a long moment.*]

Get back in your grave, Danny. I'm sorry.

[*The* SECOND MAN *approaches* RAY, *who backs warily away. He
reaches out and draws his fingers over* RAY's *face leaving marks
of white ochre.*]

[*Screaming*] Uh! No!

[*The* SECOND MAN *dances away, laughing, as* RAY *frantically
wipes the marks away with the cloth. The* SECOND MAN *dances
around him, taunting him.* RAY *raises his shotgun once more, but
is suddenly blinded by sand.*]

Ahhh ...

[*He fires wildly. The* SECOND MAN *laughs and continues to dance
as* RAY *draws his pistol and fires again. The* SECOND MAN *exits.*
RAY *clears the sand from his eyes and remains standing as lights
crossfade to morning. The wind dies and is replaced by morning
noises.* DAVID *lies unconscious by a waterhole, still wearing his
feathered shoes, now much the worse for wear.* RAY *is surrounded
by spent cartridges. He sees* DAVID.]

Christ.

[RAY *approaches warily and nudges him.*]

Danny?

[DAVID *stirs and rolls over.* RAY *sees he is unhurt and reassesses
the situation. He slings the radio to the ground and drinks.*]

Hey.

[RAY *nudges him again.*]

Hey. Dave?

[DAVID *stirs, looks up at* RAY, *then starts.*]

DAVID: Ra —

[DAVID *dissolves into a coughing fit. He washes his mouth out in
the waterhole.*]

RAY: Where is he?

DAVID: Ray. What ... ? How'd ... ? How did you ... ?

RAY: Where is he?

[*Pause.*]

DAVID: I have no idea.

RAY: Where the fuck is he? You tell me where he is.

DAVID: I don't know. We split up ...

RAY: [*levelling the shotgun at him*] Don't fuck around! If I blew your fuckin' head off who would know? Eh? So listen to me: I'm warning you. Alright? [*Indicating the waterhole*] You couldn't find this water by yourself: he must've brought you. I knew that: it's why I'm here. So where is he?

[DAVID *stares at him.*]

You're trying me, Dave. You're really fuckin' trying me. God, he's a clever little cunt. He set a trail he knew I'd get out and follow. When I got back to the car he'd let the tyres down, put sand in the tank ... Completely fucked it. He's clever. But he's got more than he can chew this time.

DAVID: Ray, I swear to you: I don't know where he is.

RAY: Then how'd you get here? You been here before?

DAVID: I ... no.

[RAY *laughs.*]

RAY: You're a fuckin' white man, Dave. A fuckin' white man. I got more blackfella in me than you'll ever have. So I'm gunna ask you once more, and you better fuckin' tell me: where is he?

DAVID: I don't know, Ray.

RAY: [*pointing the gun at him*] Bull*shit*!

DAVID: I don't! I don't! I ... don't know how I found this place.

RAY: Bullshit!

DAVID: No ... It was like ... a man, a spirit ... showed me and —

RAY: [*interrupting*] No! No!

DAVID: He was real, an ancestor, I don't know. I swear to you: he touched my face; he took my hand. As close to me as—[*'... you are now. '*]

RAY: [*interrupting*] No! No! No! Don't give me that bullshit. That spooky Aboriginal bullshit. I don't want to hear it!

[*They stare at one another.*]

[*Nastily*] I don't want to know.

[RAY *lowers the gun, turns away to wash his face in the waterhole.*]

Thing is, Dave, you think I'm the villain ... You think I'm the villain, but I'm not. I'm just a bloke that ... wants to do his job. Poppy's the villain, getting people into the ... the blackfella way, the old way, try'n'a drag it all out when a clean break is what they need. It's being caught in the *middle*'t fucks you up.

[*Pause.*]

When my dad was a copper he used to go in the camps with the Aboriginal Protection blokes and take the kids away. Just take 'em away so they never even knew about their culture or the Dreamtime or whatever. And you know what? I reckon there's value in that. There's value in it ... I don't hate Aboriginal people, Dave. Just the opposite. Just the oppostite.

[DAVID *sees a chance and makes a lunge for* RAY's *gun. He's too weak and sore, however, and* RAY *easily overcomes him.*]

DAVID: You going to shoot me now?

RAY: Me? I'm not a killer, Dave. Not like some.

[DAVID *stares at him.*]

DAVID: Don't go on, Ray.

RAY: Have to.

TJULPU: [*off, singing*]

Larrpitupi! Yinka, mantarringu, palunyalukula wakamarra kulatangka.

['*Shit! Sing, laugh, he's the one we're going to spear.*']

RAY: That's him.

[RAY *holds the shotgun ready.*]

DAVID: Ray ...

RAY: What? He's coming back with me.

TJULPU: [*off, singing*]

Yinka, yinka! Wantiyirralalaka ngananpa kulata yankutjaku parrpakutjaku, parrawitjanjaku larrpitupi! Yinka!

['*Sing, sing! Let all our spears go flying, spinning. Shit! Sing!*']

[TJULPU *appears, clutching his spear.* RAY *laughs.*]

Yinka, yinka! Wantiyirralalaka ngananpa kulata yankutjaku parrpakutjaku, parrawirrtjaku. Larrapitu! Yinka!

['*Sing, sing! Let all our spears go flying, spinning. Shit! Sing!*']

RAY: Well, well.

[*He takes his handcuffs and tosses them to* DAVID.]

Put these on him.

DAVID: No.

RAY: Do it or I'll shoot him. I'm serious. You got thirty seconds.

[DAVID *rises painfully and hobbles towards* TJULPU. *He stops as he hears singing.*]

MANNGA: [*off, singing*]

Larrpitupi! Yinka, mantarringu, palunyalukula wakamarra ku-latangka.

[*'Shit! Sing, laugh, he's the one we're going to spear.'*]

POPPY & MANNGA: [*off, singing*]

Yinka, yinka! Wantiyirralalaka ngananpa kulata yankutjaku par-rpakutjaku, parrawitjanjaku larrpitupi! Yinka!

[*'Sing, sing! Let all our spears go flying, spinning. Shit! Sing!'*]

[MANNGA *and* POPPY *appear. The* FIRST *and* SECOND MAN *dance on, remaining around the edges. All have spears, which they rattle against their woomeras. All continue to sing.* RAY *raises his shotgun.*]

RAY: Dave ... You're my witness, Dave, whatever happens. You'll tell 'em, won't you? How it was.

DAVID: Ray, let me talk to them. Everybody. Poppy —

RAY: [*interrupting*] No, fuck it. Eh, Poppy: what you doing here?

POPPY: [*indicating* TJULPU] Meet up this fella.

DAVID: [*to* RAY] Let it go.

RAY: No. [*To* POPPY, *indicating* TJULPU] That one: I take 'im lock-up.

POPPY: Wiya. You: finish.

DAVID: Ray ... stop, just ... think for a second. Think about what you're doing.

[*The Aborigines draw back their spears.*]

POPPY: [*to* RAY] Finish.

RAY: You tell 'em, Dave.

[RAY *grabs the shotgun by the stock and wields it like a club. He rushes at* TJULPU *and the two fight.* RAY *is speared in the leg by* MANNGA, *then in the side by* TJULPU. MANNGA *prepares to administer the* coup de grâce. DAVID *throws himself across* RAY.]

DAVID: No! Enough!

POPPY: Finish this one.

DAVID: No. Not finish. Enough. Poppy, enough. Spear him, you spear me too.

TJULPU: [*angrily*] Pungkulala palunya yarra. Palunyaku kututu puli pirinypa. [*'Let's kill him and go. His heart is like a stone.'*]

DAVID: No. Ngayulu wiyana ngaanya wantitiku ngaangka yulirritjaku.

[*'I can't let this one die here.'*]

MANNGA: Ngaapanuru wiya? Paluru nganapa warun kamangu. Palaru wati tjuta pungkupayi tjantu pirinypa. [*'Why not? He's our enemy. He treats men like dogs.'*]

DAVID: I can't. Ngayulu walpala wangku wayilatja palangka. Tjana kurranyku pitjaku walawala. Nyuntu ngaawanatjaku tiiwarriwa. [*'I'll call the whitefellas on the radio. They'll come pretty quick. You have to be far away by that time.'*]

POPPY: You not angry. Tjatu nyuntu mukunypa? Nyuntu walpala pirinyparrun. [*'Where is your anger? You're acting like a whitefella.'*] You: blackpalla, watpalla?

DAVID: Ngyulu ngurrpa! [*'I don't know!'*] Poppy! I'm just a fella. Just a fella.

[*Pause.* POPPY *stares at him, then suddenly turns angrily and stalks off.* MANNGA *turns to follow.*]

MANNGA: Tjulpunya, pitja ngayulawana. [*'Tjulpu, come with me.'*]

TJULPU: [*to* DAVID] Ngayulu wiya nintipuku. Ka ngayulu yanku. [*'I don't understand. But I'll go.'*]

[TJULPU *hesitates, then heads off.* MANNGA *exits.* TJULPU *pauses.*] Tjinguru nanta piruku nyaku. [*'Maybe I'll see you again.'*]

DAVID: Hope so.

[TJULPU *exits.* DAVID *picks up the shotgun, looks at it, pulls the trigger. It's empty.*] Ray ...

[DAVID *goes to the radio.*]

RAY: Dave! Dave ... don't call 'em.

DAVID: Ray ...

RAY: Don't call 'em, Dave. Please. I'm —

DAVID: [*interrupting*] I'm going to call them.

RAY: No! Dave!

[DAVID *hesitates.*] I think ... more better this one, eh?

DAVID: You want to die, then ... then die, Ray. I don't care. I don't care; but don't tell *me* to let you off the hook. Because I can't. I'd like to, but my hands are tied. I'm just doing my job. Aren't I, Ray?

[*Crossfade to later in the day. Lights up on the living room of the doctor's house, day. The action in the two locations is simultaneous: events at the waterhole are watched on television by* LES,

KATE *and* SARAH. CHARLIE *stands by the window next to his coat, briefcase, backpack and bedroll. His map and other possessions have been packed up.* KATE *clutches an overnight bag and sits next to several suitcases.* LES *sits near her, just out of reach. The room has taken on a temporary feel. As they watch several police arrive at the waterhole and, under the gaze of* FARRELLY'S *camera,* DAVID *is helped off. Two police lift* RAY, *unconscious, onto a stretcher.* BILLY *hovers by his side.*]

BILLY: Ray? Eh, boss. Ray?

[BILLY *stares hopelessly as they carry* RAY *off. He and* FARRELLY *follow.*]

GORDON: [*voice over*] ... Inspector Oaks said the constable then ignored instructions and pursued the two men into the desert.

OAKS: [*voice over*] Obviously it's ... a very ... unfortunate situation, but it does seem at this point—and I stress, at this *point* ... that the officer took the law into his own hands.

GORDON: [*voice over*] Will action be taken against the Aboriginal men?

OAKS: [*voice over*] Ah ... well ... it's too early to make a judgement on that.

GORDON: [*voice over*] Do you think the fact they're Aboriginal might affect ... how they'll be treated by other police?

OAKS: [*voice over*] No, no. No, they'll ... receive ... exactly the same treatment as any other Australian citizen under Australian law.

[*Suddenly the power goes off in the doctor's house. The image of the waterhole blacks out. A blustery wind beats around the house.*]

LES: What happened?

SARAH: The generator.

LES: Oh.

SARAH: Little goodbye present.

[*She stares out.*]

I'm sure I've left something in the surgery.

LES: I think—I think we should all ... stay here until the plane arrives. That's what they said to do.

[*Pause.*]

[*To* CHARLIE] Can you see anyone?

CHARLIE: No. Policeman. With a shotgun. Walking. Dust.

[*Pause.*]

God, what a place.

[*Lighting change: desert night throughout.* CHARLIE, SARAH, LES *and* KATE *remain still.* POPPY, *the* FIRST *and* SECOND MAN *appear seated around the spinifex fire as at the head of the play. The* SECOND MAN *holds the pack of cards.*]

POPPY: Politpalla, they been looking, looking, [*Pointing in several directions*] that way, that way. Long time. Politpalla say they finish: they die.

ABORIGINAL VOICE: [*off*] Eh! We ready now. You come dancing, eh?

SECOND MAN: Yeah, we coming. [*Holding up the cards, to* POPPY *and the* FIRST MAN] One more, eh?

FIRST MAN: [*to* POPPY] They finish, eh? Mannga, Tjulpu.

POPPY: Finish? No. They been too clever. [*Pointing*] They been that way, Mannga's country.

SECOND MAN: [*crossing his wrists*] You: they put you this one?

[POPPY *laughs.*]

POPPY: No, I been witness. I don't do nothing.

ABORIGINAL VOICE: [*off*] Eh, we ready. You come now.

SECOND MAN: Yeah, we coming!

[*The* SECOND MAN *deals out the cards as* TJULPU *and* MANNGA *enter.* TJULPU *enters the living room and passes between the stationary figures. He and* MANNGA *move into the desert, past the three card players and off. The three players throw down their cards.* POPPY *wins.*]

POPPY: [*delighted*] Ah! Big money!

THE END

www.currency.com.au

Visit our website to:

- Buy your books online
- Browse our full list of titles, from plays to screenplays, books on theatre, film and music, and more
- Choose a play for your school or amateur performance group by cast size and gender
- Obtain information about performance rights
- For students, read our study guides
- For teachers, access syllabus and other relevant information
- Sign up for our email newsletter

The performing arts publisher

www.ingramcontent.com/pod-product-compliance
Lightning Source LLC
Chambersburg PA
CBHW040054100426
42734CB00044B/3307